How to Cook with Miso

How to Cook with Miso

Aveline Tomoko Kushi

with the assistance of
REBECCA GREENWOOD
SHERMAN GOLDMAN
LILLIAN BARSEVICK
OLIVIA OREDSON
and many other friends
too numerous to mention

Japan Publications, Inc.

© 1978 in Japan by Aveline Tomoyo Kushi

Drawings and Illustrations by the Author

Published by
JAPAN PUBLICATIONS, INC., Tokyo, Japan

Distributors:
UNITED STATES: *Kodansha International/USA, Ltd., through Harper &*
Row, Publishers, Inc., 10 East 53rd Street, New York, New York 10022.
SOUTH AMERICA: *Harper & Row, Publishers, Inc., International Depart-*
ment. CANADA: *Fitzhenry & Whiteside Ltd., 150 Lesmill Road, Don*
Mills, Ontario M3B 2T6. MEXICO AND CENTRAL AMERICA: *HARLA*
S. A. de C. V., Apartado 30–546, Mexico 4, D. F. BRITISH ISLES:
International Book Distributors Ltd., 66 Wood Lane End, Hemel Hemp-
stead, Herts HPZ 4RG. EUROPEAN CONTINENT: *Boxerbooks, Inc.,*
Limmatstrasse 111, 8031 Zurich. AUSTRALIA AND NEW ZEALAND:
Book Wise (Australia) Pty. Ltd., 104–8 Sussex Street, Sydney 2000.
EAST AND JAPAN: *Japan Publications Trading Co., Ltd., 1–2–1,* THE
FAR *Sarugaku-cho, Chiyoda-ku, Tokyo 101.*

First edition: December, 1978
Second printing: July, 1979
ISBN 0–87040–450–4

Printed in U.S.A.

This book is dedicated with love and gratefulness
to my teachers, George Ohsawa and Lima Ohsawa,
to my husband, children and all the friends who
have lived with us over the past ten years.

Why Health?

When we examine the sun through a dark atmosphere and a fog of gross vapours, we do not see it clear and bright but submerged and misty, with elusive rays. Thus, when the body is turbulent and surfeited and burdened with improper food, the lustre and light of the soul instantly comes through it blurred and confused, aberrant and inconstant, since the soul lacks the brilliance and intensity to penetrate to the minute and obscure issues of active life.

PLUTARCH

Foreword

In my long and blessed life I have dined with many memorable people—kings and presidents, congressmen and senators, poets and playwrights, philosophers and seers, judges and scientists, saints and sinners. But the most unforgettable dinner guest I ever met is the lovely Japanese lady who wrote this book.

One stormy evening in the winter of 1967, Mrs. Kushi came to my home in New York with her husband. She was tinier than I and immaculately turned out in her beautiful *kimono*. I knew the Kushis then only by reputation, but I had heard they were as careful about what they ate as I had always been. So I worked with my German cook to prepare a traditional Japanese dinner. We began with miso soup. My friendly fish man Sol had brought me a shad he had caught and boned with his own hands. We served it *tempura*-style along with brown rice and vegetables.

Mrs. Kushi was delighted with our version of miso soup. She admired the dinner. She rarely ventured to eat anybody's cooking except her own, and told us what a treat this was for her. She tasted a morsel of fish and expressed great appreciation of its delicacy. Then, with her chopsticks she transferred the remaining pieces of fish from her plate to her husband's, imperceptibly without saying a word. But I noticed, and Mr. Kushi noticed.

"My wife is much more strict about what she eats than I am," he explained. Mrs. Kushi blushed faintly, lifting her hand to her face. "But I must be," she smiled. "I have five children. I never know when I may be pregnant again. By the time I discover I am pregnant, three, four or six weeks might have passed. The first weeks are so important. I must be careful never to eat anything not right for this new life inside me."

I have told that story hundreds of times and I appreciate this opportunity to tell it again. We often say the hand that rocks the cradle rules the world. In Japan, a baby is considered to be nine months old at birth. Its first cradle is the mother's womb. The hand that rocks that cradle—is the hand that rules our world or ruins it.

An increasing number of children are brought into existence each year deformed and retarded. We may be approaching the point where healthy children are becoming a minority group. Government or medical science cannot save us.

We can only save ourselves if women can liberate themselves and can accept personal responsibility for the future of their children, as Mrs. Kushi has shown us where it begins. Let us be grateful for this opportunity to learn from her.

GLORIA SWANSON
Boston

Preface

When we first came to this country about 25 years ago, there were almost no good-quality whole foods available. We had to make do with products like Quaker Oats, buckwheat groats, and a few things that we could find in Oriental food stores like buckwheat noodles and seaweed. We lived in New York near Columbia University. We could order one keg of *Hatcho Miso* once or twice a year from Japan in order to obtain the essential nutrients necessary for those who don't eat very much animal food. I am very grateful for Kyuemon Hayakawa's several-hundred-year tradition of strong miso in Japan.

Today, the importation of miso from Japan to the United States must be at least 10,000 times what it was 25 years ago. We are able to enjoy high-quality miso like barley miso, rice miso, brown rice miso, and others.

However, my real hope is that America will now begin to produce its own miso from grains grown here on this soil. I hope that each region of this country will eventually develop food production and methods of food processing appropriate to its own local climate. The only competition that would then exist between the various regions would be the competition to see who could produce the best quality food and not who could produce and sell the greatest quantity.

Eight years have already passed since I started to write this book about cooking with miso: time passess like a flying arrow. It is our dream, and our expression of gratitude, to root our macrobiotic way of life in this American continent for people's health and happiness. I decided to write this book to help people use miso in everyday life, since miso is one of the essential keys in changing from a diet of animal food to one of more healthful and peaceful food—grains and vegetables.

My very admired friend, Miss Gloria Swanson, heard this and sent me a wonderful introduction for the book through her friend, Mr. William Dufty. I had to put the miso book aside during our busy years of continuous education and establishment of macrobiotic enterprises. Meanwhile, Gloria Swanson was getting younger and more beautiful. She married William Dufty, and together they have been actively working toward the betterment of people's health. One of their remarkable projects is the introduction of whole foods into the public school lunch program.

During this time, Mr. William Shurtleff put great energy into studying miso and other Far Eastern agricultural products, traveling to Japan, and publishing *The Book of Miso*.

Over the past four years my husband started to give seminars in many European countries as well as in Central and South America. I joined him, giving cooking classes. We met many wonderful people. These experiences gave me new energy to reopen and finish this book.

I am very grateful to Rebecca Greenwood, who is now teaching macrobiotics in Colorado, for her time and energy typing and writing the English for this book in the very beginning. At our Gardner Road house, surrounded by rich greens and quiet days, while Rebecca was typing, I began drawing the pictures, which I hadn't done since my college days.

Three years later Lillian Barsevick helped to further organize the book, mixing and stirring and adding warm pressure. Finally, with her gentle touch, Olivia Oredson took it form its dark storage room for us to taste. Please make fresh, wonderful miso soup. It is now certainly enough fermented!

AVELINE TOMOKO KUSHI
Brookline, Massachusetts

May 1978

Contents

Introduction

First Encounters with Yin and Yang

In western Japan, near the Sea of Japan, in a lovely region of lakes, lies the peaceful city of Matsue. It is here that Lafcadio Hearn, a great Western interpreter of Japan, lived and even today his home is carefully preserved. A five-hour drive southward into the mountains leads to the place where I was born. I can still visualize the times when as a child I saw the steam locomotives climb the gently rolling mountain, panting and chugging. The city of Hiroshima can be reached by a five-hour drive from my birthplace, in the opposite direction. The northern side of the mountains toward the sea and toward Matsue is called San-Yin. The weather there tended to be cloudy, dark, and cold. The southern side toward Hiroshima, where the sun was usually shining, is called San-Yo. (*Yo* is the ancient Chinese word for "yang.")

About 80 years ago, the seed of Christianity was dropped into this small mountain village. In the year I was born, a Christian church with a high, Western steeple was built in the middle of the village, giving it somewhat of an exotic atmosphere. Both my parents were extremely devout Christians, and were brave enough to be the first in that region to be married in a Christian ceremony. Although they were very poor, they managed to create a very peaceful household. Both my father and mother always carried a Holy Bible with them. At that time the Bible was still largely unknown in Japan; and when my father first entered military service, he was put into a military stockade for having one. He was a good soldier, though, and so was released and permitted to carry and read his Bible. My name, "Tomoko," means "God with me." Every year, at home and in church, the stories of the Old and New Testaments were repeated over and over, so all of us children came to know them by heart.

In February 1950, I went for the first time to George Ohsawa's private school near Tokyo, and stayed and studied there for a year and a half. The school had two names, "Maison Ignoramus," and also "Student World Government Association," and published a newspaper regarding world government. The purpose of the school was to develop the understanding of yin and yang.

About one week after entering Maison Ignoramus, I showed my diary to Mr. Ohsawa. I had written several pages in a notebook. The book was returned to me with the first page covered by a single large, merciless "X." This "X" was written with a pen and here and there on the paper the point

15

had gone through, making a hole. No doubt he had scored this mark using all his strength.

I wondered how my paper could be so much in error. I had only recorded simply and sincerely my feelings upon entering the school and had given this to him. I had written:

> "When one goes to a Christian church, it is said that everyone is a 'child of *sin*,' and one begins to feel attacked by this word 'sin' which is so often and randomly used. Here, in the same way, everything is referred to in terms of Yin and Yang. In those words, Yin and Yang, there is something of the bad odor of organized religion."

If a weaker-willed and less stubborn person had received such a grade, I wonder what would have happened. But I, being somewhat insensitive, merely remarked to my friend, "Never before in my whole life have I received such a grade, and besides, there are holes in the paper!"

But I realized that the purpose of this school of George Ohsawa's, the Maison Ignoramus, was entirely for the understanding of yin and yang. Later, I also started to use yin and yang in regular conversation, without any resistance.

After about a one-year period had passed, in the spring of 1951, I was walking by myself in back near the Ohsawas' house. There was a beautiful hill, and mustard greens with beautiful yellow flowers were growing there, and also fresh green sprouting wheat plants. As I was walking there on that beautiful spring afternoon, I realized that all phenomena, the whole universe surrounding me, is just moving according to yin and yang. I realized this very deeply, in the bottom of my heart. At that moment, it was just as though on a pond covered with ice, the ice had cracked and started to melt; or, as when throwing a small stone against big rocks, it makes a sharp cracking sound—it was during those few moments of deep feeling when these vivid insights came.

From that time on, I became so happy. I wrote down in my notes a few sentences describing my opinions, and showed them to George Ohsawa as usual every day. It was generally George Ohsawa's daily practice to wake up around 2 or 4 A. M. in the morning, and during those early hours he checked all his students' reports or answered letters or read books. The day after I handed in that note, he gave me permission to depart to the United States.

At George Ohsawa's school, it was my job to sell the newspaper which they were producing at the school. Its title was "World Government." I graduated from newspaper sales because I kept the highest record of sales in the street and at the station—it was in itself a great education for me. Of course I could tell many other stories of this job; but when I made the highest record of sales was when I was eating George Ohsawa's so-called

16

*Number Seven Diet.** Then, George Ohsawa bought a ticket for me from Tokyo to New York by boat and Greyhound Bus.

During the time I was staying at the Maison Ignoramus, I did not study any macrobiotic cooking, and of course I had not studied any other aspects of natural healing either. From that basis I came to this country, the United States, and studied those things here from the beginning.

In Japan we were using the words yin and yang in everyday conversation from the time of babyhood, so in my case I already knew the words themselves. Even so, I had resistance to begin using them as we learned at George Ohsawa's school. But for you, seeing the words yin and yang for the first time, you may feel very strange when beginning to use them. After you start to use them, however, you can see that they are really based on human common sense and are easy and convenient to understand. They are like magic spectacles which enable us to find out and see things clearly.

The important thing is that this is a tool, and whenever we use it, it becomes more and more sharpened and valuable.

There are many ways to study this order of the universe, yin and yang. The best practice is for your daily life, in the kitchen. I think you will find yin and yang are very helpful in your life.

Many books and publications are available now to give you a good start, and by reading them, you can find enough knowledge to guide you. But truly, your best teacher will be the foods you cook and the implements you use. Your rice and onions, carrots and salt, your cutting knives and pots will prove to be your best teachers. And if you listen carefully to their silent lessons you will be able to develop your intuition and to make your family and yourself happy and beautiful.

---

* *Number Seven Diet:* Introduced by George Ohsawa this is a regime composed of 100% cereal grains, for the purpose of changing the direction of one's health, usually followed only for a short time. Whole brown rice is especially recommended in this regime. Those who wish to try the *Number Seven Diet* are advised to have experienced instruction.

Know the strength of man,
But keep a woman's care!
Be the stream of the universe!
Being the stream of the universe,
Ever true and unswerving,
Become as a little child once more.

Know the white,
But keep the black!
Be an example to the world!
Being an example to the world,
Ever true and unwavering,
Return to the infinite.

Know honor,
Yet keep humility.
Be the valley of the universe,
Ever true and resourceful,
Return to the state of the uncarved block.
When the block is carved, it becomes useful;
When the sage uses it, he becomes the ruler.
Thus, "A great tailor cuts little."

LAO TSU, *Tao Teh Ching*

Preparation for Cooking

Please enter my kitchen—I welcome you.

The last time Mr. Ohsawa visited the United States he stayed at our house. One day he said to us with a big smile, "I have found the definition of happiness: it is the realization of one's eternal dream."

His simple words impressed me deeply, because after studying macrobiotics and eating good food I had discovered the road of life is open; it is possible to realize one's dream. And, the very purpose of cooking is to create happiness through the realization of this dream. Thus, I offer you this book not only because it contains cooking techniques, but because I hope that it might help you find your own true happiness.

While studying in George Ohsawa's macrobiotic dormitory in Tokyo, I started to discover the importance of food and its preparation. However, during my stay I did no cooking, as I felt unqualified to enter the kitchen. Then when Mr. Ohsawa sent me to the United States, it was here that my cooking education truly began. I have studied with Mrs. Lima Ohsawa during her visits to the United States, and I have also gained experience from cooking for my husband and five children, plus from teaching and guiding the many young Americans who have studied macrobiotics in Boston.

If you are a beginner, the first few times you use these recipes it may be helpful to abide by recommended measurements; but after that, please do not limit yourself to such a mechanical approach, but try to develop your intuition.

Cooking is an excellent barometer of your physical, mental and spiritual conditon, as each dish you prepare is a reflection of yourself. Even though you prepare rice daily, it turns out differently each time. To improve your cooking it is very helpful to reflect on and strive to understand your condition. By judging the taste, balance, and appearance of a meal and noting how your family feels after eating it, you can determine your condition.

You have, also, a great teacher beside you every day: that is your own mirror. You can see any time the good or bad results of your cooking reflected in your face. Of course, you need to know a little Oriental diagnosis, but you can see easily that sometimes your nose becomes red, or that you have dark circles under your eyes, or some other sign of imbalance. When you wake up every morning, please see the mirror first, and check any difference from yesterday—it will give you a grade on your cooking!

And, although it sounds amazing, you can change your condition through cooking. Simply concentrate on the food, on its preparation, and in the largest sense, on what you wish to accomplish. Indeed, what a wonderful opportunity it is to cook for the nourishment and development of others. When cooking with this larger view, cooking is not a chore, but a positive and happy experience.

Here are some suggestions that might be helpful:

Before entering the kitchen, wash up, put on a fresh apron, and tie your hair up if it is long. It is better not to wear perfume while cooking—it interferes with your discrimination among the aromas of the foods. Similarly, listening to loud music while cooking would interfere with the sense of hearing; cooking itself has very many nice sounds like the sizzling of vegetables, steaming, and simmering, and by the sounds you can also tell how the cooking is going on.

A clean, well-ordered kitchen, with your utensils in convenient locations, is conducive to fine cooking. Maintain the cleanliness and good atmosphere of the kitchen by cleaning up as you cook, or just before you serve the meal. Allow yourself enough time so you can cook peacefully and be in harmony with your environment. Approach your cooking with both humility and the pride of a true artist, and with this attitude your love will flow into the food you are cooking and bring much happiness to others.

Start with a clear mind. Put aside all your problems and worries and simply *be* in the kitchen, with your full energy devoted to the meal preparation. Of course everyone has many troubles, small and big—but put those things aside from your mind and try to forget them completely while you are cooking. Many Zen masters teach practices to attain "nothingness" or "Mu"—but if you study cooking, that is an excellent approach to those things. By putting aside your troubles and cooking with a clear mind, your cooking becomes better, and after you eat, everyone becomes more peaceful.

Organize the menu and schedule. For example, plan when to put up the rice and when to soak the sea vegetables, so the cooking flows smoothly and the dishes are ready simultaneously at meal time.

Consider everyone's condition, and your own, and cook the meal accordingly. The atmosphere and season also determine what you choose to make and how you prepare it. Cook for the following day, as today's food creates tomorrow's energy. Thus, if someone is planning a trip or has special studies to complete, cook to prepare him for these events.

Do not strive to become a "good cook" or try to change food according to your own ego. Rather, think of the native qualities of each food. A cook should be like the conductor of a fine orchestra, trying to bring out all the inherent harmonies and order in the foods, their natural taste and power. Food is really your life—it has great power.

Cook simply. It is not so advisable to mix many things. Get to know each ingredient, its personality, how it tastes and smells, and the effect it has on daily health. Some people mix ingredients that produce unusual colors, smells, and tastes, and often use spices to cover up the unsatisfactory product. The best cooking, on the other hand, enhances the natural taste and color of each food.

The most important thing of all is—cook with love. See clearly what it is you are trying to accomplish, and with concentrated care and patience you can achieve those results. Think of each person who will eat your food and how this food will sustain him and help him to realize his happiness.

If you have a husband or boyfriend, it can make a great improvement in your cooking. That is the best way to start to learn cooking— if you have someone you really want to cook for.

Balancing Health and Diet with Miso

Balancing our food according to our condition, the season, the climatic region, and the whole surrounding environment is most important for our daily physical, mental, and spiritual condition. Our day-to-day condition accumulates, making our life more and more happy, or more and more miserable. For the past several years, besides lecturing, my husband has been giving many people dietary recommendations, privately or sometimes in a group. During lecture tours in some of the European countries, over 100 people have gathered for his group consultations. He talks with people of all ages, with all kinds of health problems—one by one, patiently and kindly—he takes time to explain how to deal with everyday food.

More than 10,000 people in the United States and European countries have come to him for advice. Among them, we see many people who are able to follow his suggestions; they become healthier and happier. Because of these experiences, he formed his Standard Dietary Suggestions. If you would like to know these recommendations and the philosophy in detail, you may read *The Book of Macrobiotics* published by Japan Publications, Inc. Here is simple standard dietary advice, as my husband describes:

Dietary Proportions

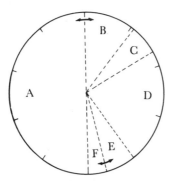

With Animal Food

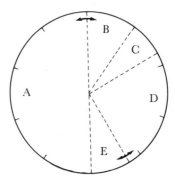

Vegetable Quality Only

A. Whole cereal grains
B. Legumes, seeds
C. Soup
D. Vegetables: ancient, modern, and sea vegetables
E. Animal food, preferably fish and seafood, or primitive land animal
F. Fruits and nuts

A. Whole cereal grains
B. Legumes, seeds
C. Soup, representing ancient seawater, with sea salt, enzyme or bacteria, and sea vegetables
D. Vegetables: ancient, more cooked, and modern, less cooked
E. Fruits and nuts, as well as raw modern vegetables and pickles

Arrows show interchange and flexibility among neighboring categories.

The proportion shown in the chart at the opposite page indicate the generally recommended amounts of the principal food and supplementary foods, as described in the list that follows:

1. *Principal food,* namely cereal grains, and their products—such as bread, chapati, noodles and pasta—from the beginning to the end of the meal. Beans and seeds, since they are near to the cereal species, could be used also as a part of the principal food, or with the dish of principal food. For example, beans could be cooked or served together with rice and other grains; and sesame seeds together with sea salt roasted and crushed, can be used as a condiment for the dish of grain.

2. *Soup,* consisting of sea vegetables with or without fish flavor, and sometimes including land vegetables, beans or grains, is to be served as the first portion of side dishes. Such soup, especially containing sea vegetables and fermented enzymes with slightly salty taste, is actually a condensed form of the ancient sea within which early life evolved before the formation of land.

3. *Land vegetable dishes,* containing leafy, ground, and root vegetables, cooked in various forms, such as sautéing, steaming, boiling, baking, and frying (when we use oil, it should be of vegetable quality) —to be served as the second part of side dishes. Vegetables of more ancient origin should be cooked more, and those of more recent origin may be cooked less and may be occasionally taken in uncooked form such as salad or pickles, according to environmental conditions and personal need.

4. *Seaweeds and water moss* cooked separately or together with some land vegetables or beans—can be served as the third part of side dishes. These seaweeds and water mosses can be served in soup as the first part of side dishes.

5. *Fish, seafood and other animal food,* if required—can be taken as part of the second part of side dishes, together with land and sea vegetables, because of their complementary and antagonistic relation in biological development. However, as mentioned before, more primordial animal life is preferred.

6. *Fruits and nuts,* chosen locally according to season, may be the last course of side dishes or last supplement to the entire meal, which may be occasionally taken as dessert either in fresh, cooked or dried form in the case of fruits, and roasted with sea salt in the case of nuts.

7. *Beverage*—as a last part of the entire meal, may be taken together with dessert or alone when required. Such beverage usually should be made of modern herb plants but occasionally could be made of ancient plants and sea vegetables. However, such fermented bever-

23

ages as alcoholic beverages may be taken in small volume before the meal if the first part of side dishes is not soup containing fermented enzymes, to smooth appetite and digestion.

Using miso in soup is the ideal way to use it every day. This is advisable for any condition, for any kind of person. The amount of miso and the kind of vegetables to use in the soup vary according to individual condition and the season. Generally, people with a yin type of condition can make a more yang type of miso soup, with more yang vegetables or sometimes fish flavor. A yang type of person can make a more yin, light-tasting miso soup.

Special Suggestions for Using Miso

1. *Wild Vegetables with Miso.* Wild vegetables give us great strength and energy. If you pick them yourself you really appreciate their strength. Such vegetables as dandelion, cattail, burdock and others usually have a strong, naturally wild taste. If you cook them with miso, the wild taste becomes more mild and more enjoyable. Also, if you make a mistake in picking wild vegetables or have inadvertently mixed in some other not-ideal-to-eat vegetables, cooking them with miso neutralizes their toxins. (Except, of course, strongly poisonous wild plants; these you must know and avoid. Mushrooms, especially, are dangerous; you must know them well.) The strong wild greens like chives, wild carrot greens, dandelion greens and others, when sautéed with miso, can give you great vitality.

2. *Miso in the Wintertime.* On cold winter days, dishes cooked with miso can prevent you from feeling cold. Or, if you catch a cold, they can help you to recover your strength and health. An especially good dish is soft rice cooked with *daikon*, *kombu*, fried *tofu*, lotus root and miso. If you are very yang or have a slight fever, you can also add dried mushrooms, cooked softly and finished with miso; this can give you great warmth. When there is a snowstorm, this is an ideal breakfast which can help to prevent catching a cold.

3. *Miso for Vitality.* Generally, for sicknesses caused by yin, you can use miso soup, soft rice with miso, and sometimes cook some other side dishes with miso such as *koi-koku*, and also use condiments like *tekka* and scallion miso. Vegetables of the onion family, including scallions and chives, are especially good cooked with miso or soft rice; they make a very good-quality dish. It is especially good for vitality to serve *mochi* together with soft rice miso soup. Toast the *mochi*, and before serving, put in soft rice miso soup. This is recommended for the winter season.

4.   Summertime Cooking with Miso.   In the summertime, when lighter cooking is appealing, you can make a delicious salad dressing or sauce using miso with lemon or with good-quality natural rice vinegar or apple cider vinegar. This keeps you from feeling too hot and gives you a nice lift on a hot day.

5.   For Bedwetting.   For a child who wets the bed, *mochi* miso soup is very good. You can serve the child a light miso soup with *mochi* in the evening to help his condition.

6.   For a New Mother.   For a mother who has just had a baby, miso soup with *mochi*, and also *koi-koku*, give her strength to recover more quickly, and also help in producing milk for breastfeeding.

7.   For Tobacco Toxication.   Miso soup is good for relieving the effects of tobacco toxication, or too much smoking. In the old days in Japan, the long tobacco pipes were often washed in miso soup. It was said that this made them very clean.

8.   After Taking Too Much Alcohol.   The morning after drinking too much alcohol, miso soup is very effective for restoring energy and clear thinking.

9.   For Burns.   When you burn your skin, if at that time you don't have any *tofu* or green vegetables available to apply to the burn, you can use miso as a healing paste.

10.   Food for Traveling.   Miso is very easy to carry with you when you travel, go backpacking or on a picnic. The miso may be dried by roasting it in a skillet over a low flame to make it even lighter. To use, simply mix with hot water, or eat together with other foods. It is also helpful to carry several varieties of miso condiments.

The yin-and-yang charts that follow show several examples to help you determine your condition and your family's condition. They may help you in choosing the most appropriate foods and cooking methods.

Yin and Yang in the Vegetable Kingdom

	Yin ($\bigtriangledown$) Centrifugal	Yang ($\bigtriangleup$) Centripetal
Environment:	Warmer, more tropical	Colder, more polar
Season:	Grows more in spring and summer	Grows more in autumn and winter
Soil:	More watery and sedimentary	More dry and volcanic
Growing direction:	Vertically growing upwards; expanding horizontally underground	Vertically growing downward expanding horizontally above the ground
Growing speed:	Growing faster	Growing slower
Size:	Larger, more expanded	Smaller, more compacted
Hight:	Taller	Shorter
Texture:	Softer	Harder
Water content:	More juicy and watery	More dry
Color:	Purple—blue—green—yellow—brown—orange—red	
Odor:	Stronger smell	Less smell
Taste:	Spicy—sour—sweet—salty—bitter	
Chemical components:	More K and other yin elements	Less K and other yin elements
Nutritional components:	Fat—protein—carbohydrate—mineral	
Cooking time:	Faster cooking	Slower cooking

Examples of Yin and Yang

Attribute	Yin ($\bigtriangledown$) Centrifugal Force	Yang ($\bigtriangleup$) Centripetal Force
Tendency	Expansion	Contraction
Function	Diffusion	Fusion
	Dispersion	Assimilation
	Separation	Gathering
	Decomposition	Organization
Movement	More inactive, slower	More active, faster
Vibration	Shorter wave and higher frequency	Longer wave and lower frequency
Direction	Ascent and vertical	Descent and horizontal
Position	More outward and peripheral	More inward and central
Weight	Lighter	Heavier
Temperature	Colder	Hotter
Light	Darker	Brighter
Humidity	More wet	More dry
Density	Thinner	Thicker
Size	Longer	Smaller
Shape	More expansive and fragile	More contractive and harder
Form	Longer	Shorter

26

Attribute	Yin (∇) Centrifugal Force	Yang $(\triangle)$ Centripetal Force
Texture	Softer	Harder
Atomic particle	Electron	Proton
Elements	N, O, K, P, Ca, etc.	H, C, Na, As, Mg, etc.
Environment	Vibration . . . Air . . . Water	Earth
Climatic effects	Tropical climate	Colder climate
Biological	More vegetable quality	More animal quality
Sex	Female	Male
Organ structure	More hollow and expansive	More compacted and condensed
Nerves	More peripheral, orthosympathetic	More central, parasympathetic
Attitude, emotion	More gentle, negative, defensive	More active, positive, aggressive
Work	More psychological and mental	More physical and social
Consciousness	More universal	More specific
Mental function	Dealing more with the future	Dealing more with the past
Culture	More spiritually oriented	More materially oriented
Dimension	Space	Time

What Is Miso? (Comment of Michio Kushi)

Miso is a fermented, aged soybean purée. It contains living enzymes which aid digestion, and provides a nutritious balance of natural carbohydrates, essential oils, vitamins, minerals, and protein.

According to Japanese mythology, miso was a gift to mankind from the Gods, to assure man's health, longevity and happiness. Miso has been an important food in the Orient since the beginning of its civilization, and now is becoming a popular food in the West.

The attributes given this food from the traditional point of view are expressed in the following song, handed down for generations, which was sung when miso was being prepared in a country home.

Song of Miso

Soybeans, being sweet and warm,[1] calm down ki,[2] by relaxing the organs, and activate ki by releasing a hundred poisons.

Koji,[3] too, being sweet and warm, enters the stomach, diminishes overeating and stagnation, opens the blocks, passes healthy energy, and circulates new blood.

Soybeans, koji and cold salt[4] are very powerful, like the devil carrying an iron club:[5] like a preacher with a drum.[6] Led by salt—heart, kidneys, lungs, spleen and liver work all together harmoniously, calming down the blood energy. Muscles and bones become smooth, dissolved poisons disappear. Blood becomes cool and dry, all pains and aches disappear. Thus sound appetite naturally arises from the refreshed blood.

Miso, being a harmonious quality between two warms and one cold, becomes cool as it meets heat, and becomes warm as it meets cold. It softens the strong, strengthens the weak, relaxes the fierce, solidifies the loose. It halts the waste of the blood and ki, driving out sick accumulations. It thus brings health and peace, freedom and spirit.

The nature of miso is plain and the quality is mild. But if it is thought to be only a supplement of food, it is a great mistake. Needless to say, miso as food is not only full of nourishment but also a wonderful medicine for various pains, tumors, and external injuries like cuts. Do spread miso over a sick place, then burn a big moxa[7] and the cause of disease disappears, pain ceases miraculously, without spoiling any part of the skin.

Therefore, to win the battle and to defend a fortress, as well as to keep a peaceful home, the storing of miso is indispensable. If a fire threatens a house and there is no time to make clay mud,[8]

---

1. *sweet and warm:* in this case they represent yin.
2. *ki* (Japanese, or *chi* in Chinese): energy, or electromagnetic energy.
3. *Koji:* Fermented rice or barley used in making miso.
4. *cold salt:* solid salt which has a feeling of cold. In this case it represents yang.
5. *devil carrying an iron club:* according to an Oriental fairy legend, a devil is supposed to carry a big iron club with which he crushes an enemy.
6. *a preacher with a drum:* sects of Buddhism, like Hokke-shu (sect) or Nichiren-shu (sect), practice preaching and praying to the rhythmical beat of a drum.
7. *moxa:* made of a special wild mugwort grass and used as a burning substance, applied on points of acupuncture meridians to treat many sicknesses. This practice has been widely exercised throughout the Far Eastern countries as one popular medicine for thousands of years.
8. *clay mud:* prevents the spread and penetration of fire, and has been used widely as wall-paste for houses; especially, for a storage house in which valuable things were kept.

28

paste miso on the window frames. Even great fire cannot penetrate through miso.

All in all, having always a stock of miso, and enjoying miso soup and miso pickles, is the life of kings and lords. Those who have no miso are really the miserable poor.

Thus, the value of this ingenious food is explained traditionally. But what is its value from a nutritional point of view?

The main ingredient of miso is soybeans. And soybeans contain approximately 34% protein, 31% carbohydrates, and 18% fat. They have nearly twice as much protein as meat or fish and eleven times as much as milk. In addition, soybeans are rich in calcium, phosphorous, iron and other minerals, and lecithin. They contain in nearly maximum proportions the amino acids essential in man's diet.

For thousands of years man has known that some foods, when fermented, are nutritionally superior to those found in their original form.

While the Western world ferments milk to produce different kinds of cheese and yoghurt, the Eastern world ferments soybeans to produce, among other foods, miso.

The carbohydrates in soybeans are less easily assimilated by the body than the carbohydrates of other beans. However, the structural change caused by miso's fermentation allows the body to use these carbohydrates with no difficulty.

Some specific health benefits of miso are:

—High in minerals for proper body metabolism.

—For heart disease, miso contains linoleic acid and lecithin, which dissolves cholesterol in the blood and softens the blood vessels. Thus miso can be of great help in preventing arteriosclerosis or high blood pressure.

—For beauty, nourishes the skin and blood to promote cell and skin tissue building. This makes your skin and hair glow with vitality.

—For stamina, miso contains large amounts of glucose which give us energy.

—It helps prevent diseases such as allergy and tuberculosis.

—For poor digestion, use miso with a garnish.

Soybeans, which originated in the East, are now being grown on a large scale in the United States. And, we are fortunate to have top-quality domestic soybeans readily available. In fact, the domestic supply is so large that many beans are exported or used for non-food products such as insecticides.

Although many food products are being invented to utilize the soybean, often these foods are highly processed and of questionable food value.

The soybean has found a home in the West. Might we not look to the East for a method of soybean preparation that has proved to be beneficial for thousands of years?

I am happy that my wife is able to present to you a cookbook in English with instructions for homemade miso, and recipes for its use in other dishes. And it is our wish that you will become well acquainted with miso, for it can help you create lasting health.

(Poem translated from *Miso Daigaku* by Mr. Kan Misumi)

味噌汁の作り方

Chapter 1

How to Use Miso for Soup

Before Japanese families adopted the American breakfast of toast and eggs, Japanese children awoke to the aroma of miso soup. It was served practically every morning, and often in the evenings as well. It imparted strength and a sense of well-being and was believed to insure longevity.

Morning miso soup generally is made more simply than evening miso soup, spring water being used as a base. In the evening a richer soup may be prepared, often with a stock base and occasionally utilizing animal products.

In general, the vegetables for miso soup should be so well-cooked that they "melt" in your mouth and after you chew well can be swallowed simultaneously with the broth. Because miso contains living bacteria which aid digestion, it is not boiled, since boiling would destroy these bacteria. The flavor of miso soup is also much more enjoyable if it is not boiled, so avoid reheating it but, if at all possible, make it fresh each time you serve it.

Various types of miso soup are made from vegetables, fish, seaweed, beans, and grain. A few examples are detailed in the next chapter. You may vary each recipe by changing the stock, the method of cooking, the vegetables, or the kind of miso used.

Selecting Your Miso

In making soup, miso may be used much like a traditional, natural bouillon cube. The miso itself makes the body of the soup; you don't need any special techniques or materials. In fact, you can enjoy a simple soup made only with the miso itself: simply boil water, and season with miso. If your miso is of a good, naturally-processed quality, it will make an excellent broth all by itself.

Care should be taken in selecting good miso when you go shopping. On the general market, various kinds of commercial miso are available which are not of the best quality. Some of these misos are fermented only two to three months, and the fermentation process is unnaturally adjusted. The use of those kinds of miso does not encourage good health—and in fact, may cause your health to deteriorate in the long run from ingesting the poor-quality ingredients.

We are carrying misos that are made with good-quality natural ingredi-

33

ents, using natural fermentation processes for the fully-required lengths of time: *Hatcho Miso*, made from 100% soybeans with salt; *Mugi Miso*, made with fermented barley, soybeans and salt; and *Aka Miso*, made with fermented rice, soybeans and salt. These varieties of miso can be enjoyed separately, or you may use two varieties mixed together to create a wide range of tastes in the soups and other dishes you cook.

You can enjoy miso soup in its simplicity, just adding a little touch of vegetable, and perhaps a contrasting garnish. By adjusting the simple ingredients according to what is available in season in your region, and according to your own health requirements, miso soup may be varied and enjoyed in every season the year round. Miso is very convenient, and once you start to use it, I think you will find it's very satisfying.

Basic Methods of Preparing Miso Soup

In this book, many varieties of soup are described: some are very rich, some are simple; some contain only vegetables, and others include grains and special ingredients. In the following paragraphs I would like to offer a simplified description of several basic cooking methods for miso soup. I hope you will enjoy using these methods to create soups suitable for your particular requirements. There is a glossary at the end of the book if you do not understand certain terms, or need more information about the types of vegetables used.

(1) *Simple Miso Soup*
Made with a broth, perhaps including seasonal vegetables simply boiled in the soup, generally without the use of oil or sauéing. Miso is added at the end. A garnish is attractive. This kind of soup is especially enjoyable made fresh for breakfast.

(2) *The Layer Method*
This type of soup is made with several kinds of vegetables—two, three, or more. The vegetables are sliced in pieces of the same size for uniform cooking time. If you have plenty of time, you can make large slices which take longer to cook; if you don't have very much time, you can make very small slices and cook them more quickly. Any style of cutting may be used.

Layer the vegetables in the pot according to yin and yang—the more yin vegetables on the bottom, the more yang vegetables on top. For example, if you are using celery, cabbage, onion, and carrot, place the celery—the most yin—on the bottom; then the cabbage, then the onion, and finally the carrot—the most yang—on top. Then, add just enough cold water to reach almost to the top of the vegetables; cover, and cook until the vegetables become a little tender. Then, you can add more water or soup stock to make the desired consistency, and cook all the ingredients together again. (When you add more water, pour it in at the side, very quietly and gently; do not simply splash the water into the middle of the soup, as this tends to disturb the vegetable layers.) Add miso at the end of cooking, and when you are ready to serve the soup, mix the vegetable layers together well.

For this style of cooking, if you would like to include grains or beans in the soup, simply wash the grains or beans and place them as the top layer, with the vegetables underneath; and, as described above, add water to almost—but not quite—cover. Then, when the grains or beans expand during cooking, just add more water. The yin energy rising during cooking helps to make the grains and beans soften—you may be surprised how easily they become soft.

In this style of cooking, you may use oil if you wish: simply brush the pan with oil before adding the soup ingredients. With or without oil, this layer method of making soup offers the opportunity for endless variations.

(3) *Sautéed Vegetable Miso Soup*

The soup vegetables can be sautéed very well to take out their raw, sharp taste; this we call making the vegetables more yang with heat. Brush a little oil in the heated soup pot and sauté the vegetables in the order from most yin to most yang. Add water and cook, seasoning with miso at the end. This makes a richer-tasting soup that is very delicious, and can also be recommended for making excellent winter stews.

(4) *Boiled Vegetable Miso Soup*

The soup vegetables are boiled separately and then combined in the soup pot with additional water to complete the cooking, before adding miso. This makes a smooth, somewhat light soup—it has a very pleasant taste and is suitable in almost any season of the year.

(5) *Miso Soup with Animal Food*

If you wish to include fish, eggs or other animal food, these may also be added to miso soup. Delicious egg miso soup or fish miso soup makes an energizing and attractive dish. Cooking methods may vary according to the kind of animal food used. Several examples are described in the next chapter.

Soup Stock

When vegetables are sautéed, their flavor becomes richer, so a stock is not necessarily required. But for broths or for summer soups, when vegetables are simply boiled, a soup stock is recommended. The following are only guidelines to be adapted as you see fit.

Kombu Soup Stock

You will find this easy-to-make sea-vegetable stock a reliable friend, as its unique flavor complements so many dishes.

> **3-inch piece of kombu (approximately)**
> **1 quart water**

Leaving the salt (white powder) undisturbed, dust all the sand off the *kombu*. Place the *kombu* in water and heat. Just before the water boils, remove *kombu*. The *kombu* may be cooked later as a vegetable dish; it should not, however, be used as a soup vegetable, since it does not become tender, except by long cooking, and absorbs too much taste from other vegetables in the soup. For a richer taste the *kombu* may be soaked for five minutes before cooking.

Vegetable Soup Stock

Don't discard wilted vegetables or vegetable parts such as carrot tops, cabbage hearts, etc. Save them, and when you have a good collection you can make a delicious stock that imparts a unique flavor to any soup. Pea hulls, corn husks, vegetable cores, tough outer leaves and squash peelings work fine. However, avoid greens that lend a bitter taste, such as spinach or

Swiss chard. Stock vegetables, if re-cooked with *tamari*, also make tasty side dishes, after you have used them to make a stock as follows:

Vegetable parts, cut into small pieces
Water to cover

Boil 5 to 10 minutes.

Dried Vegetable Soup Stock

For soups requiring a sweeter-flavored stock, use dried vegetables such as dried *daikon* or dried-out root vegetables.

1/2 cup dried vegetables
5 cups water

Wash, then soak vegetables in water for 5 minutes. Bring to a boil, and cook for 3 minutes. Then remove vegetables and re-cook them as a side dish.

Dried Mushroom Soup Stock

Although mushrooms make a delicious stock, please use them with moderation because they are yin vegetable, and be sure to balance the rest of your meal with an appropriate form of yang.

2 dried mushrooms, medium size
1 quart water

Soak the mushrooms in water for 5 minutes. Remove from water and cut them into small pieces. Since the tip of the stem is fibrous and often contains sand, remove the tip and discard it. Place the mushrooms into the water again and bring to a boil. Reduce the flame and simmer for 5 minutes. Strain out the mushrooms which then may be used in cooking another dish.

   Place vegetables in a soup pot, add water, bring to a boil, and simmer uncovered for 5 minutes. Strain.

Grain Soup Stock

This is a favorite stock in some Zen monasteries.

1/2 cup grain, dry toasted
1 quart water

Place grain in cold water, bring to a boil and cook for 2 to 3 minutes. Strain. The grain may then be used in bread, *tempura* or baked dishes.

Soup Stock Using Animal Food

If you are vegetarian, you may not want to use fish or any other animal food in your cooking; but if you like to use fish on special occasions, you will find it goes well with miso too. Any type of fish, shellfish, or fish bones may be used for soup stock, as well as wild birds or other kinds of animal food.

In the Orient, bonito is traditionally used to make soup stock; it harmonizes easily with vegetable flavors. Bonito makes an excellent soup—you may enjoy trying it with miso.

Bonito and Kombu Soup Stock

Bonito fish flakes give a delicate fish flavor and add body to the soup.

3-inch piece of kombu
1 quart water
3 tablespoons bonito shavings (fresh bonito imparts a richer flavor)

Dust any sand off the *kombu*, place it in water and heat. Just before water boils, remove the *kombu*, and bonito shaving, and boil for 1 minute. Remove from fire and strain. The bonito flakes may be served with the *kombu* as a side dish.

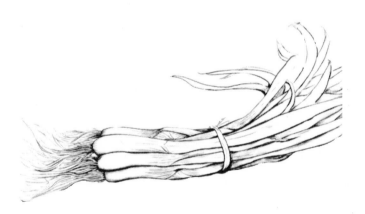

Sea Vegetables in Miso Soup

For someone unfamiliar with the taste and texture of sea vegetables, *wakame* in miso soup is an easy introduction to sea vegetables. Dulse may also be used in miso soup, and *nori* is a favorite garnish.

Miso soup, containing a sea vegetable, can be likened to the ocean from which we have evolved. For miso creates the salty fluid which nurtures us as the internal ocean of our bloodstream, and sea vegetables are one of the most ancient forms of life.

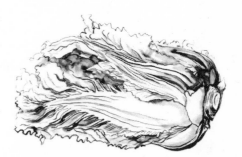

Washing Vegetables

When washing root vegetables, such as *daikon*, carrots, burdock, etc., first scrub them with a vegetable brush making sure that all of the soil is removed from the root, then rinse them off under cold water.

When washing large green leafy vegetables, wash each leaf separately to make sure that all soil is removed and that no insects stick to the leaves.

One of my students was washing watercress by just rinsing the whole bunch of watercress under cold running water without bothering to separate the leaves. I explained to her that the proper way to wash watercress was to fill a pot full of water, place the watercress in the water and separate each stem, then to proceed to wash each stem individually. As I was washing the watercress again the proper way, a small baby eel swam out of the watercress in the pot of water. This is why it is very important to wash the vegetables very carefully. You should wash the vegetables very carefully, change the water in the pot and then rinse them again to be sure that they are thoroughly cleaned.

When washing leeks, I slice the root in half, as much soil sticks to the inside of the root. Then I proceed to wash each section separately.

Sometimes broccoli has tiny green insects on the flowerettes that look just like part of the broccoli flowers. So be very careful to wash the stalks very well. If soil sticks to the leaves and roots of the vegetables, this is a very good sign. You can be sure that they are very healthy, strong vegetables. Supermarket vegetables do not have soil sticking to them. These vegetables are not ideal. They have been sprayed and washed many times.

In Japan when I was a child we used to wash the vegetables in streams of running water.

If you pick vegetables from a garden yourself, always remove old stems and leaves, and parts of the vegetables that you will not be able to use in the kitchen may be returned to the garden to decay into the soil.

Cutting Soup Vegetables

Start with a good vegetable knife, a clean cutting board and any vegetables, such as a carrot; then discover how many ways you can show off this simple vegetable to its best advantage. Vegetables may be cut in an infinite variety of shapes and sizes.

Cutting vegetables is an art and can be learned quickly. The size and shape of vegetables and seaweed govern the time they will need to cook.

Several factors influence the way to cut a vegetable for a given dish. If you and your family or friends eat with spoons rather than with chopsticks, cut the vegetables into small pieces.

Cut each type of vegetable into the same sized pieces to ensure even cooking.

When you have considerable time to cook, cut vegetables in large pieces and cook them for a long time until they are very tender. Soup vegetables should be so tender that they melt in your mouth.

Cut soup vegetables into shapes that complement your meal; for example, if a side dish contains large vegetable rounds, then you might choose to cube or dice the soup vegetables.

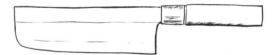

Garnishes

Garnishes are a functional art, for they not only make a soup appear more appetizing, but they also improve its digestibility. A touch of garnish provides the balance necessary for easy digestion.

Suitable garnishes include chives, broken or minced parsley, squares or strips of toasted *nori*, whole or minced watercress leaves, and lemon peel shavings. Carrot rounds thinly sliced and cut into the shape of a flower make an attractive garnish. Dark sea-green *nori* looks beautiful on a soup containing white vegetables or *tofu*.

Chapter 2

Miso Soup Recipes

A life in harmony with Nature,
the love of truth and of virtue,
will purge the eyes to understand
her text. By degrees we may come
to know the primitive sense of the
permanent objects of nature, so
that the world shall be to us
an open book, and every form
significant of its hidden life and
final cause.

RALPH WALDO EMERSON

All the following recipes are for six normal portions, unless otherwise stated, and are for soups made with or without oil, as desired. When sautéing the soup vegetables, I recommend using dark sesame oil. It has a strong flavor, so normally I just brush a very small amount in the pan. It is best to use a heavy iron or stainless steel pot, rather than a thin pot, for making miso soup.

Simple Miso Soup

Onion Wakame Miso Soup

This soup is such a favorite here in Boston and so easy to prepare that many of our friends have it very often.

1 ounce dry wakame
1 cup thinly sliced onions
1 quart stock or water
1/2 cup miso
Oil for sautéing

Soak the *wakame* in cold water until soft. Cut into ½-inch pieces. Add the soaking water to the stock if it is not too salty; otherwise, use it later for preparing rice or vegetables. Sauté the onions, placing them evenly in the pan. Add *wakame* and enough stock to cover the vegetables. Bring to a boil, reduce flame and cook until very tender. Then add remainder of stock, bring to a boil, and again reduce flame.

Place miso in a bowl or *suribachi*, add ¼ cup broth and purée until the

43

miso is completely dissolved in the liquid. Add to the soup pot and simmer for 5 minutes.

Creamy Onion Miso Soup

The whole onions in this soup open up to look like delicate lotus blossoms, and they become tender enough to melt in your mouth.

> **6 whole, medium-sized onions**
> **3 tablespoons diced onions**
> **1 quart stock or water**
> **3 tablespoons whole wheat flour**
> **1/2 cup miso**
> **1 teaspoon minced parsley**
> **Oil for sautéing**

Make three vertical slashes from the top and halfway down each whole onion. Sauté the diced onion. Place the whole onions (cut side down) over the sautéed onions. Reserving 1 cup of stock, cover the whole onions with remaining stock and cook until onions are soft, but not so soft that they will fall apart.

While onions are simmering, toast flour in remaining oil until brown, then let cool. Mix flour with last cup of stock to make a paste. Stir into soup and cook until thick, stirring gently to avoid breaking the onions. Place miso in a bowl, add ¼ cup broth and purée, then add purée to soup and continue to simmer for a few minutes, or until ready to serve. Garnish with minced parsley. (When using *kombu* as a stock, omit the oil and flour.)

Daikon Miso Soup

In Japan, *daikon* is one of the favorite miso soup vegetables. Since *daikon* stores well, farming families have *daikon* miso soup frequently throughout the fall and winter. The taste of this vegetable complements miso. When cooked in soup it becomes soft without losing its shape.

> **1 cup daikon, sliced into thin rounds**
> **1 quart stock or water**
> **1/4 cup miso**
> **1 sheet toasted nori**
> **Oil for sautéing**

Sauté the *daikon*. And enough stock to cover the vegetables; bring to a boil. Add remainder of stock, bring to a boil, reduce flame and simmer until vegetables are tender. Place miso in a bowl, add ¼ cup broth, and purée. Add purée to soup and simmer for 5 minutes.

Toast *nori* by holding it over the flame until its color turns from black to green. Tear toasted *nori* into small pieces and use as a garnish with each serving. *Nori*, like all seaweeds, is full of important minerals.

Chinese Cabbage Miso Soup with Dumplings

Dumplings make any soup a treat, especially for children. Miso soup with dumplings is so satisfying that it almost makes a meal in itself.

1 cup sweet rice flour
1/4 cup boiling water
2 cups shredded Chinese cabbage
1 quart stock or water
1/4 cup miso
Oil for sautéing

Place flour in a bowl, add boiling water, and blend. Knead for 5 minutes, then mold dumplings into any form you wish, of ½-inch thickness. Set aside.

Sauté the cabbage. Add enough stock to cover the vegetable and bring to a boil. Cover pot and simmer until cabbage is tender. Add remainder of stock, bring soup to a boil and drop the dumplings into the soup. When dumplings rise to the surface, they are cooked. Reduce flame. (You may also cook the dumplings separately and add.) Place miso in a bowl, add ¼ cup broth, and purée. Add purée to soup and allow to simmer for a few minutes. Garnish with parsley.

Celery Miso Soup

Celery is not a common vegetable in Japan, but when I came to America, I was happy to discover that this popular Western vegetable is very much at home in miso.

1/2 cup celery, cut into 1-inch pieces
1/2 cup thinly sliced onions
1 quart stock or water
1/4 cup miso
Oil for sautéing
1 sheet toasted nori

Sauté celery and onions. Add enough stock to cover the vegetables and bring to a boil. Add remainder of stock, cover pot, and cook until vegetables become tender. Place miso in a bowl, add ¼ cup broth, and purée. Add purée and allow to simmer for a few minutes. Garnish with *nori*.

Zucchini Miso Soup

2 cups zucchini, cut in 1/2-inch slices
1/2 cup thinly sliced onions
1 quart stock or water
1/4 cup miso
Oil for sautéing
1 thinly sliced carrot cut into flower shapes

Sauté onion, then zucchini. Add stock. Bring to a boil, lower flame and simmer without a lid for 3 minutes. Cover pot and simmer until vegetables are tender.

Place miso in a bowl, add ¼ cup broth, and purée. Add purée to soup and allow to simmer for 5 minutes. Garnish with carrot flowers.

Cauliflower Miso Soup

Steaming miso soup with 1 or 2 flowerettes of cauliflower on top is a very simple yet extremely attractive dish.

1 cup cauliflower in flowerettes
1/2 cup diced onion
1 quart stock or water
1/4 cup miso
Oil for sautéing
1 sheet toasted nori

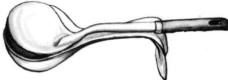

Sauté onions until transparent. Add cauliflower and stock and cook gently until cauliflower is soft yet still retains its shape. Place miso in a bowl, add ¼ cup broth, and purée. Add purée to soup and simmer for several minutes or until ready to serve. Cut *nori* into ½-inch squares and use to garnish each serving.

Sesame Miso Soup with Broccoli

Sesame seeds provide such a unique and rich flavor to this soup that you'd best prepare enough for seconds.

> **2 cups broccoli**
> **1 quart water**
> **1/2 cup toasted sesame seeds**
> **1/4 cup miso**
> **Oil for sautéing**

Separate top of broccoli from stem, and cut into flowerettes. Slice stem into 1-inch pieces. Sauté broccoli stems. Add water to cover vegetable, bring to a boil. Add all but ½ cup remaining water, cover pot; bring to a boil, reduce flame and simmer until broccoli stems are soft.

To keep tops of broccoli green, place with remaining water in a separate pan and boil uncovered until color begins to deepen. Add cooking water to soup but set tops of broccoli aside. Thoroughly grind sesame seeds in a *suribachi*. Place miso in *suribachi* with ground sesame seeds, add ½ cup broth, and purée. Add purée to soup and allow to simmer for a few minutes. Serve, floating a few pieces of flowerette in each bowl.

Burdock Miso Soup with Dulse

If you try digging up wild burdock, you will find what a strong vegetable this is, for its tree-like roots are very firmly anchored into the soil. Since burdock, which lends a unique, almost earthlike, flavor to dishes, is very yang, use it in small quantities.

> **1/4 cup shaved burdock**
> **1 cup thinly sliced onion**
> **1 quart stock or water**
> **1/4 cup dulse**
> **1/4 cup miso**
> **Oil for sautéing**
> **1 scallion**

Sauté onion, then burdock. Add enough stock to cover vegetables, bring to a boil, reduce flame, cover pot and simmer until vegetables are tender. Check dulse carefully and rinse lightly. Add dulse to soup and simmer for

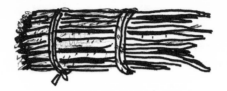

a few minutes. Place miso in a bowl, add ¼ cup broth, and purée. Add purée to soup and simmer for 2 to 3 minutes. Turn off flame.

Garnish with scallion cut in thin rounds.

Squash Miso Soup

A winter squash, such as butternut or buttercup, is recommended.

2 cups diced squash
1 quart stock or water
1/4 cup miso
Oil for sautéing
Parsley for garnish

Sauté squash over a medium-low flame for 10 minutes. Add stock, cover pot, and simmer until tender. Place miso in a bowl, add ¼ cup stock, and purée. Add purée to soup, and simmer for 5 minutes; serve. Garnish with parsley.

String Bean Miso Soup

2 cups string beans cut into 1/2-inch pieces
1/2 cup thinly sliced onions
1 cup cabbage, cut into 1-inch squares
1 quart stock or water
1/4 cup miso
Oil for sautéing

Sauté first the onion, then the string beans and cabbage. Add water to cover and bring vegetables to a boil.

Add the remaining water and simmer for 15 minutes. Place miso in a bowl, add a ladleful of soup stock, purée and add to the pot. Cover pot and simmer for a few minutes. The miso should not be boiled, merely heated; high heat will destroy the valuable enzymes.

For variety add 2 tablespoons of sesame butter or *tahini* during the last 10 minutes of cooking.

Use toasted bread squares as a garnish; add just before serving. Bread squares go especially well with onion or squash soups.

Ken Chin Soup

If you have some leftover odds and ends of vegetables and you are wondering how to use them try this recipe, which came from the Ken Chin Zen Monastery in China.

   Simply sauté the vegetables in the order given below; first heat the pan and brush with oil.

1/4 cup shaved and lightly sautéed burdock
1/4 cup sliced and lightly sautéed daikon
1/4 cup sliced and lightly sautéed string beans
1/4 cup shredded and lightly sautéed cabbage
1 cup sliced and lightly sautéed carrots
1 quart water
1/4 cup miso

Place the sautéed vegetables in a soup pot, add enough stock to cover vegetables, and bring to a boil. Add remainder of stock, cover pot, bring to a boil. Reduce flame and simmer until vegetables are tender. Place miso in a bowl, add ½ cup broth and blend until creamy. Add creamy mixture to soup and simmer for several minutes until ready to serve.

Noodle Miso Soup

Often, noodles provide a light, pleasant taste, very satisfying to your appetite. In soup they take on the soup's flavor, becoming even more delicious. Any shaped pasta may be used in this recipe, but a simple preparation of whole wheat flour, salt and water is recommended.

1/4 cup dried mushrooms
1/2 cup chopped celery
1 quart water
8 ounces cooked whole wheat noodles
1/4 cup scallion, sliced in 1-inch pieces
1/4 cup miso

Soak mushrooms in 1 cup of stock for 30 minutes. Cut into small pieces, and pour soaking water back into the stock. Sauté celery, then mushrooms. Add enough stock to cover vegetables; bring to a boil. Add remainder of stock, cover pot, reduce flame and simmer until vegetables are tender. Finally, add cooked noodles and simmer for 2 to 3 minutes more. Add scallions. Place miso in a bowl, add ¼ cup broth and purée. Add purée to soup and simmer for a few minutes.

Spiral Macaroni Miso Soup

1/2 cup onions
1/2 cup carrots
1/2 cup celery or cabbage
8 ounces cooked whole wheat spirals

Cook in the same manner as the above recipe.

Any kind of whole wheat noodles or homemade noodles can be used to make noodle miso soup.

Miso Soup with Green Peas

Fresh peas, if we keep their vibrant green color, are very beautiful in soup. Green peas are the most yin variety of beans and, therefore, are best combined with a yang vegetable, such as carrots.

1/2 cup diced onion
1/2 cup diced carrot
1 quart stock or water
1/2 cup fresh green peas
1 cup boiling water
1/4 cup miso
Oil for sautéing

Sauté onions until they are transparent. Add carrots and continue to sauté for a few minutes. Add stock or water, cover and boil until vegetables are tender.

To keep the fresh green color of the peas, drop them into boiling water and cook for 2 to 3 minutes. (Save this water for cooking grains or for soup stock.) Add peas to soup, right before putting in the miso. Place miso in a bowl, add ¼ cup broth and blend until creamy. Add blended miso to soup and simmer for a few minutes.

Grain Miso Soup

Grain miso soups are very good for lunch or for breakfast. You can create a whole menu with one dish.

Grain soups are also very good to give us energy, particularly in the winter months.

Millet Miso Soup

> 1/2 cup millet
> 1 cup sliced onions
> 1 cup butternut squash
> 1/2 cup celery
> 1 quart water
> 1/4 cup miso
> 1 sheet toasted nori

Wash millet and then roast in a dry pan.

Brush pot with oil. Layer the vegetables in the pot in the following manner: first place the celery, then the onions, then the squash. Spread the millet evenly on top of the layered vegetables. Cook over a medium flame. Add water gradually as the millet expands. Do not stir. After the millet becomes very soft then add the rest of the soup stock or water. Bring to a boil. Reduce flame. Mix miso with a small amount of the soup water, and purée. Add the puréed miso to the soup just before serving. Garnish with *nori* and serve.

Other Grains:

The following grains can be used to make soup. Prepare them in the same manner as the above recipe:

Buckwheat
Rice
Barley
Cracked Wheat
Oatmeal

You may use a variety of different vegetables with each different grain.

Bean Miso Soup

Bean miso soup can be prepared in the same manner as grain miso soup, layering the vegetables and placing the beans on top of the vegetables.

Lentils, kidney beans, pinto beans, and many other kinds of beans are suitable for this method.

If you wish to use very hard beans, it may be necessary to soak them before cooking.

Miso Soup Without Oil

If your dinner includes several dishes containing oil, you might prefer to use boiled rather than sautéed vegetables in the soup. Boiled vegetables are also more suitable for preparing a light, summertime soup. Simply place all vegetables in the soup pot from yin to yang, omit the sautéing step, add water or stock to cover the vegetables and proceed as directed in any of the previous recipes.

One or two kinds of vegetables may be used, or several. Grains, vegetables, beans, seaweed—all can be cooked without oil. Cook until tender; you will enjoy their flavor and sweetness.

Watercress Miso Soup

Wash carefully one bunch of watercress, and boil for just a minute or two in a small amount (about 1 inch) of water. Slice the watercress into ½-inch slices. Then, you can use the watercress as a garnish after the soup is done. Before you serve, just place the watercress in the soup.

Bring soup stock to a boil in a separate pot, then turn down the flame. Any type of soup stock may be used—a vegetable broth, or simply water. Place miso in a bowl, add ¼ cup broth, and purée. Add purée to soup and simmer for 5 minutes. Then, add the watercress.

Sometimes, you may also add dulse, which has an interesting color and flavor; or, toast *nori*, tear into small pieces, and use as a garnish accompanying the watercress.

Variation:

For variety, other soft green vegetables can be used, in season. Some green vegetables have a strong, bitter flavor and hard texture, and do not blend well with other vegetables. Boil the vegetables, and if the stock is sweet and not too strong in flavor, they are suitable to use. Swiss chard, soft kale, large sweet scallions, soft *daikon* leaves, soft mustard greens, milkweed, spinach, and many wild grasses are delicious.

Miso Soup with Variety

Miso Soup with Seitan

This is a quick and easy miso soup which is delicious. *Seitan* is a good source of protein, and *seitan* starch water is very good for digestion and also for nursing mothers. To obtain *seitan* and *seitan* starch water, please refer to the recipe for *seitan* on p. 55.

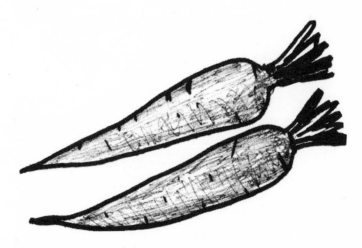

1 cup sliced Chinese cabbage
1/2 cup sliced carrot
1/2 cup fresh mushrooms, sliced
1/4 cup sliced burdock
1 cup sliced onion
1 cup sliced seitan
Spring water
**Approximately 1 cup seitan starch water (This amount depends
 on how thick you would like the soup to be. Let the seitan
 starch water settle before using, so you can take the more
 condensed part, which has better thickening power).**
1/4 cup miso
Nori, toasted and cut into pieces

Wash and cut vegetables. If there is enough time for cooking, slice the
vegetables in large pieces; if you have only a short time, use small pieces.
Place vegetables in the pot in layers, in the following order: first mushrooms, then Chinese cabbage, onion, carrot, burdock, and finally *seitan*.
Cover vegetables with spring water, level with the top of the vegetables.
Bring to a boil, then simmer until tender. It is not necessary to mix the
vegetables during cooking. When tender, add more spring water or soup
stock; bring to a boil again and simmer for a few minutes.

Slowly add the *seitan* starch water, little by little; do not add all at once.
Slowly stir as you simmer because *seitan* starch water has a tendency to
stick; or else, use a very low flame. After the *seitan* starch water has become
transparent, cook well 5 to 10 minutes longer, stirring gently. Remove a
small amount of water and mix with the miso. Add the miso purée to the
soup pot, then simmer again for a few minutes.

The *seitan* starch water may be omitted, but if you do use it, the soup
will give you more energy, and especially will make you warm in the
wintertime.

Nori makes an attractive garnish.

Basic Recipe for Homemade Seitan

Seitan is the wheat gluten or protein. It is very nutritious and easy to digest. To make *seitan*, we separate the protein from the starch and bran of the wheat. To do this, we make a whole wheat dough and knead it under water. The *seitan* or protein part, which is more yin, rises and clumps together, while the starch and bran, which are more yang, sink and dissolve into the water. The *seitan* is rinsed very well and then cooked. The easiest cooking method I have found for *seitan* is to cook it in small pieces in a pressure cooker. To make a delicious taste, you can cook the *seitan* together with *tamari*, *kombu* and a little ginger. Of course, any other vegetables may be added too.

Protein, being yin, is very good cooked with a salty taste such as *tamari*. The starch left over from making *seitan* is very nice in making a sweet taste, as in desserts.

10 cups hard-whole-wheat flour
Water

Add water to flour gradually, until the dough is neither stiff nor soupy. Knead 10 to 20 minutes; then set in a bowl, cover with cold water and let soak for 10 to 15 minutes, if you are in a hurry. If you have the time, it may be soaked longer—then, the *seitan* becomes soft more easily. Use cold water to soak if you would like to use the starch later, as warm water allows the starch to spoil more easily. (If you are interrupted at this point and must leave the *seitan* soaking for a long time, over two or three hours, be sure to leave it in a cool place.)

Begin to knead and rinse the dough under the soaking water, then pour off the water into a container to use later. Pour more water over the *seitan*, and knead again; or, you may knead under running water. It is best to rinse the *seitan* two times, although one rinse may be sufficient if you wash it well in that water. Usually, I keep the water from only the first rinse. If the large amount of dough is hard to handle, you can break it into smaller pieces and wash them one at a time.

As you knead the dough under water, it will first break up, and then will form into an elastic mass in your hands. As you continue kneading, this gluten will form into a cohesive ball.

After washing the *seitan*, form it into 1-inch balls and place in a pressure-cooker with *kombu*, ginger, and enough water to cover. Add one cup of *tamari*. Bring up to pressure and cook 45 to 60 minutes. Then allow the pressure to come down; serve as is, or use the *seitan* in other recipes.

If you do not have a pressure-cooker, the *seitan* can be boiled instead, although this takes longer and does not produce the soft, fluffy texture that results from pressure-cooking. After washing the *seitan*, bring cooking water to a boil. Meanwhile, form the gluten into 1-inch balls or larger patties. Drop these into the boiling water. They will sink, then rise to the surface when they are done. Take them out when they rise. It is also possible to boil the gluten in one large piece and slice it afterwards.

After boiling, if you wish, the patties may be deep-fried for a hearty taste. After boiling, let them drain, then pat off excess water and deep-fry. After boiling (and after deep-frying if you choose), place the pieces of *seitan* in a pot with *kombu*, ginger, water to cover, and *tamari*, and cook for a longer time than for pressure-cooking: one, two, or even three hours —the longer you cook it, the more delicious it becomes.

After cooking with *kombu*, ginger, and *tamari*, the *seitan* is ready to use in your favorite soup recipes or in a vegetable dish. Slice the *seitan* and

cook with rice, soup, or vegetables. At that time, you can adjust the taste of the whole dish—if the *seitan* is very salty, you may not need to add more salt taste to the dish. When using *seitan* in miso soup, a small amount is used, and if the *seitan* is unusually salty, less miso is used to season the soup.

There are many uses for the starch water left over from making *seitan*. If you let the water settle for 10 to 15 minutes, it separates: the milky white, heavier part sinks to the bottom and a clear water remains on top. Pour off the clear water and use the more condensed part to make gravies, cream soups and desserts. The clear part is also very good for your beauty—for washing the face and hands to make soft and smooth skin.

In Japan they make a product called *fu* by a process similar to that for *seitan*. *Fu* is very thin, baked *seitan*, sometimes formed into thin rounds like wheels. After washing the dough, instead of boiling, they bake it. *Fu* can be stored for a long time and is very easy to use. Traditionally, it is recommended for babies and sick persons. To use *fu*, soak it and cook in soup or with vegetables—it cooks quickly, in just 5 minutes. It picks up the flavors of the other ingredients, and is nice and soft and smooth.

Miso Soup with Shiitake Mushrooms and Dulse

A nice, light soup for a spring or summer day.

> **1/2 cup shiitake mushrooms**
> **1 bunch broccoli**
> **1 quart water**
> **1/4 cup dulse**
> **1/4 cup miso**

Soak the *shiitake* mushrooms in a cup of water until soft, about one-half hour; then cut off the stems and slice. If the stems are tender, mince them and add to the soup along with the soaking water. If the stems are hard, then peel off their skin and please use the inside soft part. Cut thick stalks of broccoli into 1-inch chunks. Keep the flowerettes to add at the end of the cooking period as they open up to a beautiful green flower when only lightly cooked.

Layer the vegetables in the soup pot, first the *shiitake* mushrooms, then the broccoli stems. Add water, cover and bring to a boil. Reduce flame and simmer for 30 minutes.

Add broccoli flowerettes to the soup and allow to simmer. Add dulse. Purée miso in a small amount of broth, add to the soup, and simmer for a few minutes longer before serving.

You can garnish with fresh parsley.

Mizore Soup

In Japan, the early winter rain, often mixed with sleet, is called *Mizore*. The fish, or fish stock, of this yang soup is balanced by the large amount of lightly cooked *daikon* which is yin and aids the digestion of animal food.

1/2 cup bonito stock
1 quart soup stock or water
2 cups grated daikon
1/2 cup white fish (optional)
1/4 cup miso
Parsley for garnish

Bring stock to a boil; add fish and *daikon*. Boil uncovered until the *daikon* smell has disappeared, about 2 to 3 minutes. Turn down flame. Place miso in a bowl, add ¼ cup broth, and purée. Add purée to soup, allow to simmer for 5 minutes. Garnish with parsley.

Fish Dumpling Miso Soup

1 cup sliced daikon ·
1 quart stock or water
1 cup white fish fillet
1 pinch salt
1/4 cup whole wheat flour
1/8 teaspoon grated ginger
1/4 cup miso
1 finely sliced scallion

Place *daikon* in pot, add enough stock or water to cover, and bring to a rapid boil. Add remainder of stock, cover pot, and simmer until *daikon* is soft.

Mash fish in a *suribachi* with a pinch of salt. Mix in flour and ginger, and from this mixture make dumplings 1 inch in diameter. Drop dumplings into boiling soup and when they rise to the surface, reduce flame. Place miso in a bowl, add ¼ cup broth, and purée. Mix purée with soup and allow to simmer for a few minutes. Garnish with scallion.

Oyster Miso Soup

1/2 cup shelled oysters
1 quart stock
1/4 cup miso
1 teaspoon shaved lemon rind
1 minced scallion

Wash oysters well. Bring soup stock to a boil. Drop in oysters and cook 5 minutes. Turn down flame. Place miso in a bowl, add ¼ cup broth, and purée. Add purée to soup, simmer several minutes until ready to serve. Garnish with shaved lemon rind and scallion.

Egg-drop Miso Soup

1 fresh fertile egg
1 quart stock or water
1/4 cup miso
1 sheet nori, toasted and cut into pieces
1 minced scallion

Beat egg. Bring stock to a boil; pour egg into boiling stock in a thin thread, stirring quickly all the while. (If you do not stir, the egg will clump together in the pot.) The thread of dropping egg cooks quickly and rises to the surface of the soup, like tiny beautiful flowers. Boil 2 to 3 minutes longer, then turn down flame. Place miso in a bowl, add ¼ cup broth, and purée. Blend purée with soup and simmer a few minutes. Garnish each bowl with *nori* and scallion.

Rice and Scallion Miso Soup

This makes a good wintertime breakfast; you'll feel warm all day.

1 ounce dry wakame
1 quart water or stock
2 cups sliced scallion (includes minced roots)
2 cups cooked brown rice
1/4 cup miso
1 sliced scallion

Rinse off *wakame* quickly and soak until soft. Remove from soaking water and cut into ½-inch pieces.

Place 2 cups scallion and *wakame* in pot, and add enough stock or water to cover. Bring to a rapid boil. Add rice and remainder of stock. Cover pot, and gently simmer for 10 minutes.

Place miso in a bowl, add ¼ cup broth, and purée. Add purée to soup, and simmer for a few minutes. Garnish with scallion and serve.

Sake Lees Miso Soup

Sake lees is a by-product of making *sake*. This soup is very warming and relaxing on a cold winter night.

1 cup sliced daikon
1 quart stock or water
1/4 cup miso
1/2 cup sake lees
1 sliced scallion

Place *daikon* and stock in pot and bring to a boil. Cover pot, reduce flame, and simmer until *daikon* is soft. Blend *sake* lees with ½ cup stock in a *suribachi* and add to soup. Bring to a boil and simmer for a few minutes. Place miso in a *suribachi*, add ¼ cup broth, and purée. Add to soup and let simmer for several minutes. Garnish with scallion.

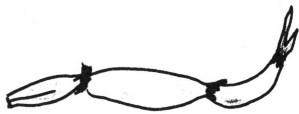

Lotus Dumpling Miso Soup

Traditionally believed to strengthen weak lungs and relieve sore throats, lotus is a very yang vegetable excellent for wintertime use. Lotus itself does not go well with miso, so here it is used in a dumpling.

1/2 cup whole wheat flour
1 cup chopped lotus
1/8 cup boiling water
1 quart kombu stock
1/4 cup miso
Several springs minced watercress

Mix flour, lotus and boiling water to form dumplings. Bring stock to a boil. Drop lotus mixture, a teaspoonful at a time, into boiling stock. When the dumplings rise to the surface, they are done. Reduce flame. Place miso in a bowl, add ¼ cup broth, and purée. Blend purée with soup and simmer. Garnish with watercress.

Mochi Miso Soup

Mochi is traditionally thought to be helpful to nursing mothers in producing good milk. A bowl of this soup in the evening is very warming.

Mochi:
2 cups sweet brown rice
1/4 teaspoon salt
2 cups water

Soup:
1 cup scallions, sliced in 1-inch pieces
1 cup sliced Chinese cabbage
1 quart stock or water
1/4 cup miso
1 sheet toasted nori

Wash sweet rice and pressure cook with salt and water for 30 minutes. Place cooked rice in a *suribachi* or bowl and pound with a wooden pestle until completely smooth and glutinous. Form into 2-inch dumplings and set aside.

Sauté scallion, then Chinese cabbage. Add stock to cover vegetables; bring to a boil. Add remaining stock, cover pot, and simmer until the vegetables are soft. Add *mochi* dumplings and cook until they rise to the surface. Place miso in a bowl, add ¼ cup broth, and purée. Blend purée with soup, and simmer. Garnish each bowl with *nori*.

Dandelion Miso Soup

Since dandelion is usually bitter, it goes best in miso soup when deep-fried and served as a garnish. The result is an extremely yang dish recommended for people suffering from general weakness. Instead of dandelion, you can use parsley or other wild grasses as well.

Broth:
> **1 quart kombu stock**
> **1/4 cup miso**

Tempura:
> **1/2 cup whole wheat pastry flour**
> **1/2 cup corn or rice flour**
> **1 cup water**
> **1 cup wild dandelion leaves and roots**

Mix flours, then add water to make a batter. Chop dandelion roots finely; cut the large greens, but leave the small greens whole. Add to batter, drop by the spoonful into hot vegetable oil, and deep-fry until golden. Drain on paper towels.

Heat stock to boiling. Place miso in a bowl, add ¼ cup broth, and purée. Add purée to soup and allow to simmer. Top each serving with 1 or 2 pieces of dandelion *tempura*. Serve immediately.

This recipe can be made with just a simple soup stock as described; or, you can use one or a combination of boiled vegetables cooked in the soup stock. Then, like a crisp garnish, the *tempura* topping complements those soft vegetables. Many kinds of *tempura* can be used. Including croutons, there are hundreds of varieties of *tempura*: grains, beans, vegetables, fish . . . be creative!

Unohana-Jiru

Unohana is the name of a small, white flower that blooms in the early summertime. For those of you who have found that homemade *tofu* is delicious but have not yet discovered what to do with the by-product lees, this soup offers an excellent use for them. It is also pleasing to look at, like a field of delicate *unohana*.

> **1/4 teaspoon oil**
> **1/2 cup shaved burdock**
> **1/2 cup sliced turnip or daikon**
> **1 quart stock or water**
> **2 cups tofu lees**
> **1/4 cup miso**
> **1 sheet toasted nori**
> **1 finely sliced scallion**
> **Oil for sautéing**

Sauté burdock, then turnip (or *daikon*). Add enough stock to cover vegetables and boil. Add remainder of stock, cover pot, and simmer until vegetables are soft. Add *tofu* lees and cook rapidly for 2 to 3 minutes. Reduce flame. Place miso in a bowl, add ¼ cup broth, and purée. Blend purée with soup and allow to simmer. Garnish with *nori* and scallions.

Tofu Miso Soup with Wakame

This is traditionally the miso soup par excellence. The soft-textured *tofu* goes perfectly in the miso.

1 ounce dry wakame
1 quart stock or water
1 cup tofu, cut into 1-inch squares
1/4 cup miso
1 sliced scallion

Soak *wakame* in cold water until it becomes soft, then remove from soaking water and cut into 1-inch pieces. Add *wakame* and *tofu* to soup stock. Bring to a boil and then simmer until the *tofu* expands and rises to the top. Place miso in a bowl, add ¼ cup broth, and purée. Blend purée with soup and allow to simmer. Garnish with scallion.

Tofu: How to Make at Home

3 cups dried soybeans
10 cups water
2 teaspoons nigari

Wash soybeans and soak overnight or for at least 12 hours in a cool place. Drain off the soaking liquid for later use. Grind the beans in a hand grain mill (or a liquifier); then force this through a cheesecloth or fine sieve. The fiber of the original bean will be retained, and a white liquid is left. The

63

leftover fiber may be used in soups, pastries, with vegetables and in muffins.

For each cup of the strained soy "milk," add 3 cups of water. These may be from the original soaking water plus additional fresh water. Slowly, bring this mixture to a rolling boil (if possible, use a double boiler, as this liquid sticks easily), and then add the *nigari*. Add only enough to begin coagulation and stir just enough to mix the ingredients. Allow the mixture to stand until coagulation stops; press it into the desired shape, and it is ready for use.

When *tofu* is to be used in dishes where it will not be cooked, it should be boiled or pressure-cooked first for about fifteen minutes.

Aburage (Deep-fried Tofu) Miso Soup

In olden times in Japan, someone returning to his mountain home and carrying a recent purchase of *aburage* on his back, often would arrive at home without the *aburage*. It would be said that a crafty fox had stolen it, because, as every child knew, foxes love *aburage*. Indeed, the temple fox guardian is given offerings of *aburage*.

**1 square tofu
1 cup daikon, in thin rounds
1 quart kombu stock
1/4 cup miso
Thinly sliced scallion**

Place *tofu* in paper towels and squeeze out excess water. Deep-fry the *tofu* in hot oil until golden approximately 5 minutes on one side, and 3 minutes on the other side. Remove from oil and drain. Whether homemade or ready-made *aburage* is used, remove excess oil by washing the *tofu* under hot water. Then pat dry and cut into thin strips.

Place *daikon* in soup pot, add stock to cover vegetables, bring to a boil. Add remainder of stock, cover pot, and simmer until *daikon* is tender. Add *aburage* strips and simmer for 5 more minutes. Place miso in a bowl, add ¼ cup broth, and purée, then add to soup, and simmer. Garnish with scallions.

Tofu Dumpling Miso Soup

Everyone loves dumplings in soup.

**5 medium-sized squares of tofu
2 tablespoons kuzu
1 quart stock or water
1 cup scallion, cut into 1-inch slices
1/4 cup miso**

64

Squeeze *tofu* in cheesecloth to extract water (discard this water). Mash *tofu* in a *suribachi*. Mix 2 tablespoons *kuzu* with 2 tablespoons cold water and then add to *tofu*. Make dumplings the diameter of a quarter and ½-inch thick. Bring soup stock to a boil, add dumplings, and cook until dumplings rise to the surface. Reduce flame, add scallions and simmer. Place miso in a bowl, add ¼ cup broth, and purée. Blend purée with soup.

Go Jiru

For miso soup with a milk-shake-like texture, try this recipe; it is especially delicious when made with freshly harvested soybeans. It is also very nourishing and good for weakness because of its high protein content.

> **1 ounce dry wakame**
> **1/2 cup dry soybeans**
> **1 quart stock or water**
> **1/4 cup miso**

Wash soybeans and soak until tender; usually 24 hours is sufficient soaking time. Drain, and add soaking water to soup stock. Grind soybeans to a fine paste in a flour grinder or *suribachi*. Lightly rinse *wakame* and soak 5 minutes. Add *wakame* soaking water to stock. Cut *wakame* into 1-inch pieces and add to stock. Bring soup to a boil, add ground soybeans, and bring to a boil again. Reduce flame and allow to simmer for ½ hour. Place miso in a bowl, add ¼ cup broth, and purée. Add purée to soup, and allow to simmer.

A delightful garnish for this soup would be parsley as it adds a fresh green color for contrast.

Jinenjo Miso Soup

Jinenjo or mountain potato grows wild in the mountains of Japan. It is an extremely yang potato and not only delicious but gives tremendous vitality. A small amount of grated *jinenjo* can be added to any of your soups.

> **1/2 cup whole wheat flour**
> **1 cup grated jinenjo**
> **1 quart stock**
> **1/4 cup miso**
> **1 teaspoon slivered lemon rind**

Mix flour and *jinenjo*. Bring stock to a boil and drop a teaspoonful at a time of *jinenjo* mixture into stock. When the dumplings rise to the surface of the stock they are done; reduce flame. Place miso in a bowl, add ¼ cup broth, and purée. Add purée to soup and allow to simmer. Garnish with slivered lemon rind.

Koi-koku (Carp and Burdock Miso Soup)

Koi-koku is especially good for a new mother, as it helps her to regain strength quickly and to produce healthy milk. A new mother can take a bowl a day for one week. This dish is used as a folk remedy for people suffering from low vitality. Weak or strong, though, everyone loves *koi-koku*, as it has a gourmet flavor.

> **3 tablespoons oil**
> **1-pound carp, whole**
> **Slivered burdock: at least the same volume as the amount of carp—after slicing, not by weight—is needed. The ideal ratio is 3 parts burdock to 1 part carp, but as carp tend to be so large in the United States, using 3 parts burdock would yield an enormous amount of soup.**
> **Water to cover**
> **1 cup used kukicha tea leaves**
> **1 cup miso**
> **2 teaspoons fresh grated ginger**

Buy a live carp and ask your fish man to remove only the gall bladder as it is very bitter.

Cut the fish into ½-inch slices, using head, scales, fins, in fact, everything. Shred the burdock roots. Put used *kukicha* tea leaves in cheesecloth and tie at the top.

Sauté the burdock in sesame oil. Add the carp to the soup pot, then add the burdock. Add the tea bag. Add sufficient water to cover and bring to a boil. Reduce flame and simmer from 4 to 8 hours depending upon the size of the fish, until the bones and scales are soft. (Or, pressure-cook for 2 hours.) If the water evaporates, add more.

When the bones have disintegrated, take out the tea bag. Purée the miso with a small amount of soup broth and add to the soup. Then gently simmer for 5 minutes. Will keep for 1 week if refrigerated or kept in a cool place.

なめ味噌

Chapter 3

Miso Condiments
and Relishes

Condiments

Miso condiments are salty seasonings sprinkled on rice and other grains. Each individual member of a family requires a different salt consumption according to his or her physiological needs, and this varies from day to day. Since no cook could prepare separate dishes for each person, first determine the average need for salt in your family and then prepare your meal with a little less than that amount. Those who desire more salt can then add that to their food in the form of condiments.

Since condiments keep well, several weeks' supply may be made at a time. Keep them on the kitchen or dining room table in wooden or ceramic covered containers.

Tekka

Traditionally-made *tekka*, which has been cooked on a low flame for 16 hours, can serve as a fortifying "medicine" for those with weak blood. Since *tekka* is a very yang condiment, use only a small amount.

1/2 cup oil
2/3 cup minced burdock
1/4 cup minced carrot
1/3 cup minced lotus
1 teaspoon grated ginger
1-1/3 cups soybean miso

Heat a skillet, add ¼ cup oil and when oil is warm, sauté the vegetables in the following order: burdock, carrot, lotus and ginger. Add the remainder of oil, and miso. Cook over a low flame for 3 to 4 hours, stirring frequently, until it is as dry as possible.

Sesame Condiment

This condiment contains fresh oil from the sesame seeds, protein from the miso, and a light touch of chives.

> **3 cups sesame seeds, toasted**
> **1/3 cup miso**
> **1/4 cup chopped chives**

Place sesame seeds in a *suribachi* and grind until 80% done. Add miso and mix thoroughly, using a light pressure. Add chopped chives and blend in thoroughly.

Chile Miso Condiment

The green pepper in this condiment gives a spicy taste. Eggplant may be substituted for green pepper for a once-a-year summertime variation.

> **Oil for sautéing**
> **1 cup green pepper, diced**
> **1 cup miso**
> **1/2 cup water**

Heat a skillet, brush with oil, and sauté the green pepper. Purée miso with water, add to green pepper, and cook slowly for at least 1 hour, until there is no extra liquid and the condiment has a tender, melting consistency.

Relishes

These easy-to-make relishes provide an artful touch to a meal. They can be put on top of the entrée or to its side, or served in a separate relish dish.

Miso Relish

2 tablespoons oil
1 cup scallion roots and greens, chopped
1/3 cup diced lotus root
1 heaping tablespoon miso
1/4 teaspoon ginger

Sauté scallion roots and greens, and then lotus; cook until tender, about 30 minutes. Add miso and simmer 5 minutes. Add ginger and cook 1 minute longer.

Sigure Miso Relish

Sigure means late autumn quiet rain. This was named by Mrs. Lima Ohsawa when she was making this relish in my home in New York.

3 tablespoons oil
1/2 cup minced onion
1/2 cup minced carrot
1/2 cup minced lotus
Small amount of water
1 heaping tablespoon miso
1/8 teaspoon ginger
Oil for sautéing

Sauté onion, carrot, then lotus. Add just enough water to cover vegetables and simmer until soft. Blend in the miso and cook for 3 minutes. Stir in the ginger and remove from fire. This relish is good on grains, vegetables, or bread.

71

Scallion Miso Relish

2 cups scallions, cut in thin rounds, and scallion roots, minced
Oil for sautéing
1 heaping tablespoon miso
2 tablespoons water

Sauté roots, then greens. Purée miso with water and gently place on top of the scallions. Cover, and cook over a low flame for 5 to 10 minutes. Mix gently and serve.

味噌ソースとバターの作り方

Chapter 4

Miso Sauces
and Spreads

The cooking of food is the highest of all human arts. It can create happiness or unhappiness, health or sickness, wisdom or ignorance, wealth or poverty, genius or foolishness, and even the higher and lower levels of humanity and spirit. The person who is in charge of cooking, therefore, occupies the central position in society, just as those who govern fire can control the world. This art is almost exclusively in the hands of woman, and her understanding and sensibility are directly transferred into her cooking. Thus, as the master of food and cooking, woman controls human destiny.

MICHIO KUSHI

Miso Sauces

Just covering a vegetable or grain with a sauce transforms an everyday dinner into a special affair.

Plum Miso Sauce

**2 tablespoons chopped umeboshi
1/3 cup miso
1 cup sake**

Blend all ingredients and cook over a slow flame for 2 to 3 minutes. This sauce should be freshly prepared each time it is used.

Variation:

Sautéed diced onions can be blended in with the ingredients.

Sumiso

Sumiso is a traditional Japanese sauce made of miso and rice vinegar. Good quality rice vinegar is preferred but if it is not available, substitute apple vinegar or fresh lemon, lime or orange juice instead.

75

2 tablespoons kuzu
1 cup water
1/4 cup miso
1 teaspoon rice vinegar or lemon juice
1 teaspoon grated lemon peel, or small amount of fresh grated ginger

Dissolve *kuzu* in ½ cup water in a saucepan. Add remainder of water and cook over a medium flame until *kuzu* is translucent. Remove from fire, add miso, rice vinegar or lemon juice, and lemon peel.

This sauce is delicious poured over steamed vegetables or rice. You can also add a green garnish such as chopped parsley or finely chopped watercress.

Renee's Miso Sauce

3 tablespoons whole wheat flour
1 tablespoon oil
3/4 cup water
1 tablespoon minced onion
1 tablespoon chopped parsley
1 heaping tablespoon miso

Sauté flour in oil until browned. Add water gradually, and when consistency is creamy and well-cooked, remove from fire. Sauté onion and parsley in a separate pan. Blend all ingredients. Serve over grain or vegetable dishes.

Miso Bechamel Onion Sauce

For a white sauce, use white unbleached flour.
For a light sauce, use whole wheat pastry flour.
For a brown sauce, use whole wheat flour.

For each quart of sauce:
1/2 cup sesame oil
2/3 cup flour
5 cups water or soup stock
1 or 2 minced onions
1-1/2 tablespoons miso
2/3 teaspoon salt
Oil for sautéing

Sauté the flour in oil, stirring constantly. For white sauce, do this just until the lumps have been dissolved; for a light sauce, sauté until the color is slightly darkened; for a brown sauce continue roasting until the color is rich brown and there is a nutty fragrance—about 10 minutes.

Let pan cool. Sauté onions separately. Slowly add the liquid and onions to the flour, stirring until the mixture comes to a boil. Stir in the salt.

Place an asbestos pad under the pot and simmer uncovered for 20 minutes. Add diluted miso and simmer for a few minutes.

In place of onions one could use scallions, watercress, leeks or minced parsley.

Spreads

For children's and adults' lunches, spreads can be put on bread or buns, and with some lettuce added these make an attractive sandwich and a nourishing one as well.

The *Miso-Tahini* spread with some chopped onion added makes a delicious sandwich spread and also is a welcome dish to serve to evening guests along with homemade bread.

My children take these sandwiches to school as an alternative to the rice ball with *nori*.

Be creative; try to make other sandwich fillings for your children. There are innumerable possibilities which are not only nourishing but very tasty too. When served with crackers and bread, spreads make a delicious snacktime food.

Miso-Tahini Spread

> **3 tablespoons tahini**
> **1 tablespoon miso**

In a dry skillet toast *tahini* over a medium flame until it begins to turn golden. *Tahini* cooks quickly and so requires constant stirring and careful watching. When it is toasted, remove from the fire and blend with miso. If a thinner mixture is desired, dilute with boiled water that has cooled. This spread enhances bread or crackers.

Variation:

Add ½ teaspoon grated orange rind with the miso.

Walnut Miso Spread

> **1 cup walnuts**
> **1/4 cup miso**
> **1/4 cup boiled water**

Toast the walnuts in a heavy skillet over medium heat until lightly toasted. Remove from heat, let cool and sliver. Place slivers in a *suribachi* and grind to a paste. Purée miso and water and blend with walnuts into a smooth cream. Serve with bread, or spread on celery sticks. This delicious spread goes well on *ohitashi* (Japanese-style boiled vegetables).

Variation:

Pecans, peanuts, or sunflower seeds may be substituted for walnuts. Or, make a salad dressing by doubling the amount of water.

Miso-Watercress Spread

Makes 1/2 pint:

> 1 bunch fresh watercress, chopped
> 1/2 cup finely chopped scallion or leek roots
> 1 tablespoon sesame oil
> 3 tablespoons water
> 2 tablespoons miso

This spread is made in the same way as the scallion-miso relish (see p. 72), but you have to cook the scallion roots a longer time so that they will become tender, making a smooth mixture.

Heat oil in a small skillet and sauté the scallion roots very well. Purée miso with water and place on top of the scallion roots. Add the watercress, cover and cook 2 to 5 minutes. Mix well, and serve on grain, bread, or crackers. For a richer spread, add a spoonful or two of sesame butter.

Of course you can use the whole scallion in this spread, but the scallion roots have a million-dollar value, so please don't throw them away. It's nice to use all parts of a vegetable whenever possible—and also, scallion roots have a special strong vitality. If you cut them off and throw them on the ground as many people do, you will see their strength: when rain comes, they start to grow again.

Parsley stems may be used in the same way as scallion roots in this spread.

Party Spreads or Hors D'oeuvres

Cut bread into canapé-size pieces and spread with any of the relishes or spreads. These can be baked if desired. You can also use crackers instead of whole wheat bread.

Arrange attractively on a large platter, garnish with sprigs of parsley and serve.

お菜に味噌のつかい方

Chapter 5

Side Dishes
with Miso

Vegetables and Miso

If you like good food, cook it yourself.
Li Lweng

Miso-Stuffed Lotus

Miso fills the hollow chambers of the lotus; when the lotus is sliced into sections, the contrast of the lotus root with the miso forms an exquisite design.

> **1 lotus**
> **2 tablespoons tahini**
> **2 tablespoons miso**
> **1/2 teaspoon grated ginger**
> **2 teaspoons minced parsley**
> **Tempura batter**
> **Vegetable oil**

Wash lotus. Boil the whole lotus for 5 to 10 minutes. Remove and cut off the ends. In a shallow dish blend miso, ginger, *tahini* and parsley. Gently pound one end of the lotus into the miso mixture until the miso fills the hollow chambers of the lotus. Place lotus on a dish and set aside for an hour. Miso mixture will draw out liquid from the lotus. Roll lotus in this liquid. Then roll lotus in whole-wheat flour. Then dip the whole lotus into *tempura* batter made from whole-wheat flour and arrowroot flour. Deep-fry the lotus in hot vegetable oil for 2 to 3 minutes or longer, if necessary. Drain, and when cool, cut into thin slices. Since this is a very yang combination, only one or two slices are sufficient per person.

Onion Flowers

6 whole small onions
2 5-inch strips of kombu
1 or 2 medium cabbage leaves
1/4 cup miso
1/4 cup water
Parsley for garnish

Make three vertical slashes through the top and halfway down each whole onion.

Place *kombu* on the bottom of a skillet with ¼ inch of water, add cabbage leaves and place onions on top. Cook with a tight lid on a low flame until soft. Turn off flame. Purée miso with water and add purée to the onions, being careful not to break the whole onions. Allow to sit covered for 5 minutes before serving with chopped parsley garnish.

Kombu or cabbage leaves may also be used alone to line the pan. You may also cook the onions by themselves, first heating the skillet and brushing it with oil, adding a small amount of water during the cooking as necessary.

Miso-Stuffed Onions

Makes 6 servings:

6 onions, medium-sized (approximately 3 inches in diameter)
1 tablespoon oil
3/4 cup miso

82

1/4 cup chopped parsley
1 teaspoon minced lemon peel
5-inch strip of kombu

Peel onions. Cut a wide circle into the top (not the root end) of the onions with a paring knife. With a spoon, scoop out the center to form a shell about ½ inch thick. Set half of the scooped-out onion center aside to use in another dish.

Mince remaining onion center. Heat a skillet, add oil and lightly sauté the minced onion. Mix with the miso, lemon peel, and parsley, and stuff the onion shells with this filling.

Place *kombu* on bottom of baking dish, add water to ½-inch depth and place onions on *kombu*. Cover and bake in an oven pre-heated to 350 degrees until the onions become soft.

Stuffed Bell Peppers

1 cup diced onion
1 cup miso-tahini spread (see p. 77)
6 small bell peppers, parboiled
Oil for sautéing

Heat a skillet, brush with oil; lightly sauté onion. Remove skillet from fire, add *Miso-Tahini* spread and blend together. Cut tops off peppers and clean out insides. Stuff with mixture of sautéed onions and *Miso-Tahini* spread, and place tops back on the peppers. Place stuffed peppers in an oiled casserole dish and add a small amount of water. Cover dish and bake in a pre-heated, 350-degree oven until very tender.

Carrot Tops and Miso

There is no need to let carrot tops go to waste. These fibrous greens are good for the teeth and also aid digestion.

4 finely-chopped carrot tops
1 tablespoon miso
Oil

Heat skillet and brush with oil. Sauté carrot tops over a medium-high flame until they are tender. If tops are fresh and young they sauté quickly; if they are tough, add a little water after several minutes of sautéing and cook until tender. Add miso and cook over a low flame for 2 minutes.

Variation:
Daikon tops instead of carrot tops are also delicious.

Ohitashi Chinese Cabbage

Ohitashi-style vegetables are cooked in boiling water for a very short time—just dipped in for 3 minutes or less. The whole leaf, rather than the cut leaf, is cooked. Vegetables that may be prepared this way are Chinese cabbage, cabbage, chicory, Swiss chard, watercress, scallions, endive, leeks, lettuce and mustard greens.

> **8 Chinese cabbage leaves, whole**
> **1 quart water**
> **1/3 cup sumiso (see p. 75)**

(see p. 75)

Place Chinese cabbage in rapidly boiling water and cook uncovered on high flame until cabbage becomes soft (about 3 minutes). Remove from water and arrange leaves in 2 stacks. (Save cooking water to use in soup stock, bread or other dishes.) Cut stacked leaves into 1-inch servings. Pour 1 to 2 teaspoons *sumiso* over each serving. Yields approximately 14 pieces and will serve 7.

Cabbage Rolls

These delicate rolls filled with tasty white and green dumplings and adorned with a miso sauce make a very attractive and satisfying dish. Do not be put off by the long instructions; actually this dish is very easy to prepare.

Makes 5 servings:

> **1/2 cup sweet rice flour**
> **1/2 cup brown rice flour**
> **1/4 teaspoon salt**
> **1/2 cup minced parsley**
> **1/2 teaspoon grated lemon peel**
> **2-1/2 cups water**
> **5 large cabbage leaves**
> **Kanpyo (gourd strip) to tie rolls, or substitute unbleached cotton thread**
> **5-inch strip of kombu**
> **1 teaspoon miso**
> **2 teaspoons kuzu**

To make the dumplings, mix flour and salt in a bowl. Blend in parsley and lemon, then add ¼ cup boiling water; mix and knead for 5 minutes. Form into dumplings 2 inches long and 1 inch wide, which can be set aside while you prepare the cabbage.

Bring remaining water to boil and place a whole cabbage in the hot water for a few seconds until the outer leaves can easily be removed. Peel 5 leaves from the cabbage head. The leaves can be made more flexible for rolling by slicing off the protruding part from the center vein (see illustration).

Soak *kanpyo* for 1 or 2 minutes until soft. Place dumpling in the center of the cabbage leaf, fold edges over, and roll into a tight bundle. Tie with *kanpyo* strip (see illustration). Place *kombu* in a skillet; place the cabbage roll on top of the *kombu*, and add the water in which the cabbage was steamed. Cover the skillet and cook over a medium flame until the cabbage is transparent. Remove from skillet, leaving excess liquid in pan. The *kombu* can be used again in making different dishes. (Add additional water if necessary while cooking the cabbage roll.)

Purée miso in cabbage water and place in skillet. Dissolve *kuzu* in cold water and mix with miso mixture. Cook this mixture over a medium-low flame until *kuzu* is translucent. Pour sauce over cabbage rolls just before serving.

Furofuki Vegetables with Sumiso

While we are eating something very hot, we are blowing on it—that is the meaning of *Furofuki*. The large, colorful pieces of vegetables create a warm country atmosphere.

Vegetables suitable for this dish are whole, small zucchini, large slices of *daikon*, carrot, burdock, turnip, parsnip or kohlrabi.

> **3 cups vegetables, sliced in 1-inch rounds—you may use only one kind of vegetable, or a variety**
> **Water to cover vegetables**
> **1 to 3 cups sumiso (see p. 75)**

Bring water to a boil, add vegetables, cover and cook until vegetables are tender. Remove from pot to serving dish and top with *sumiso*. As a variation, serve the *sumiso* separately and use as a dip.

Sea Vegetables and Miso

Wakame-Cucumber Salad

> **Makes 10 servings:**
>
> **1 ounce dry wakame**
> **2 cups thinly sliced cucumbers**
> **1 teaspoon salt**
> **5 tablespoons toasted sesame seeds**
> **1 tablespoon miso**

Wash *wakame*, then soak for 15 minutes. Cut leaves into ½-inch pieces. If stem is very hard it may be removed and used in another dish. Spread cucumber slices on paper towels, sprinkle with salt, and let sit for 15 minutes. Wipe or rinse off salt and combine with *wakame*. Crush sesame seeds well in a *suribachi*. Add miso and blend together, and gently mix with the *wakame* and cucumbers. This dish is good for summertime, in cucumber season.

Kanten with Miso and Lemon

2 sticks kanten (kanten powder may also be used)
3 cups water
2 tablespoons miso
2 lemons
Pinch of ginger

Wash *kanten* sticks lightly with cool water, pull into pieces and place in a pot with water. Put on flame, and keep stirring until all *kanten* melts, about 10 to 15 minutes or longer.

Rinse mold before pouring the *kanten* into it, for easier removal. Allow to cool.

Stir miso, fresh lemon juice and ginger in a *suribachi*. Place in a separate dish and serve with the *kanten*. This combination makes a refreshing summer side dish.

Beans and Miso

Kidney Beans with Miso

Makes 5 servings:

1 cup kidney beans
Water
2 teaspoons miso

Wash kidney beans, put in pot and add just enough cold water to cover. Bring to a boil over a high flame; reduce heat and cook with a drop-top lid until tender. As the beans expand during cooking, add cold water a little at a time as needed to cover—we call this "shocking with water." When beans are tender, dilute miso and pour over the top. Simmer another 10 to 15 minutes. It is not necessary to mix the miso into the beans as this will occur naturally as the miso goes down during cooking.

With the exception of black soybeans and *azuki* beans, you can cook almost any kind of dry beans in this way. If you are using an especially hard bean like chickpeas, you may soak them before cooking. If using soybeans, toast them first in a dry pan so that they will become soft more easily.

Baked Pinto Beans with Miso

Makes 5 servings:

> **1 cup pinto beans**
> **3 cups water**
> **3/4 cup minced onion**
> **1/4 cup miso**
> **Oil**

Wash beans and soak in water for 1 hour. Pressure cook beans in soaking water for 45 minutes. Heat a skillet, brush with oil, and sauté onion. In a ceramic baking dish combine onions, cooked beans and miso. Bake 3 to 4 hours in a 275-degree oven.

For variety, you can bake most kinds of beans in this way. Vegetables such as onions and carrots may be baked together with the beans from the beginning. They become meltingly tender, and add a sweet juiciness to the beans.

Chapter 6

Miso Pickles

Centuries of civilizations have developed ways of preparing pickles used as complementary side dishes which can uniquely enrich our daily cuisine and delight the imagination. They also provide us with nutritional balance and harmonize the digestion.

Pickles should be kept in supply year-round and served every day. They are an important source of vitamins and minerals, in a form which is easily assimilated by our metabolism. The enzymes created by aging are very beneficial for good digestion.

Misozuke

Misozuke, or miso pickles are slightly stronger than regular pickles and are good to serve more in the winter months, especially if miso soup is missing from the table.

Root vegetables such as burdock, carrots, *daikon*, kohlrabi, turnips, ginger, lotus, parsnips and celery root are excellent for this method of pickling.

Place enough miso to cover the vegetables in a crock or jar. First wash and scrub the vegetables thoroughly with a brush. The vegetables are prepared by slicing thinly; then, bury them in the miso and cover lightly. No weight on the cover is necessary. Store in a cool place. Pickles are done in three days to a week, when they are relatively soft and taste "done."

Green leafy vegetables are unsuitable because of their high water content. An exception to this rule would be watercress and the stems of broccoli. Dip the broccoli in hot water first, peel skin, then submerge in miso; they will be ready in about a week. Watercress should also be dipped first in hot water and then inserted into the miso; it will be done in 3 days to a week.

Since if you are making homemade miso, you can bury your vegetables in miso during the aging period, we hope this will encourage more people to make their own miso and in that way reap the benefits of miso and pickles at the same time.

Traditionally, miso pickles were made in the miso from barley. Vegetables are distributed throughout the crock at the start of the miso's aging period— after the third and final mixing. Then a little salt is sprinkled on top of the miso to inhibit spoilage.

If the miso is to be used only for pickling, half the keg may be filled with vegetables; however, if the miso is intended for use in everyday cooking, add no more than one part vegetables to three parts miso. When vegetables are added at the start of the miso's aging, they may be added whole, but if one buys ready-made miso for pickling, the vegetables should be sliced before burying them in the miso.

We hope you enjoy making miso pickles.

Quick Lemon-Miso Pickles

10 lemons
1/2 cup water
1 teaspoon grated ginger
1 cup miso
1/2 cup unrefined sesame oil

Mince lemon peel (insides are not used). Place in a pot, add water, and cook uncovered 5 minutes. Heat a skillet, add oil: when it has warmed, add the cooked lemon peel, miso, and ginger. Mix thoroughly and cook for 2 to 3 minutes. Cool and store in a jar for one week. Serve with rice or salad.

Red Snapper in Miso

1 pound red snapper fillets
1 teaspoon grated ginger root
Miso

Rub the raw fillets with ginger root, then bury in a keg or crock of miso. Wait 1 week. Extra delicious.

Nuka or Rice Flour Pickles

Pickles made from *nuka*—the bran of polished brown rice—have been an everyday item for generations in the East. However, since we use organic rice in its unpolished state, there is no organic bran available. Try using whole brown rice flour instead.

A pickle barrel will take only a half-hour to make and will last for years. Pickles are important because they contain lactic acid which helps maintain healthy intestinal flora, and it is only with the help of healthy flora that we can properly assimilate our food. And also—they are very delicious.

Vegetables
5 pounds nuka or brown rice flour
1 to 2 cups salt
10 cups water
1 cup mugi miso (or hatcho miso if preferred)
Kombu
Egg shells (optional—these add calcium and help neutralize
  excess acidity)

Roast the rice before grinding. If you do not have a grinding mill and are using purchased rice flour, roast at medium heat until the color changes

slightly. Cool. Boil the water, salt and *kombu* and let it cool. Place in a container. A wooden barrel is ideal but a crock or enamel bucket will work also. Mix well with *nuka* (or flour) and miso. This is now the basis of your pickle barrel.

Unused portions of vegetables, like onion skins, tied in a cloth sack and placed in the keg help yinnize the salt more quickly. After 3 or 4 days remove the cloth sack and use the contents as compost.

To the crock add vegetables which have been thoroughly scrubbed to discourage any undesirable bacterial growth. You can experiment with different types of vegetables. Firm vegetables like burdock, carrots, turnips and *daikon* seem to work best. The smaller the vegetable piece, the sooner it will pickle. Large root vegetables can be quartered or halved. Leaves, because they contain more water, should be allowed to dry a half-day before using. A small slice of carrot will be ready to eat in 2 or 3 days while a larger piece may take 1 week to pickle. Add only enough vegetables so that the vegetable surfaces do not touch each other.

Lighter vegetables such as yellow squash, zucchini and celery should be added whole to the mixture.

Remember that when you remove a vegetable, add another vegetable and in this way you will always have a supply of pickles on hand. The *kombu* seaweed can be eaten when it is soft.

Place a plate or wooden cover on top of the mixture and weigh heavily with a stone. After water rises to the top, remove the heavy weight and stir the mixture. Place a lighter weight or none at all and whenever you remove a pickle, which should be daily, stir the mixture to blend flavors and prevent mold.

With this method, the pickling mixture will remain good for a couple of years. Pickles will be ready in 2 or 3 days but the longer you leave them in the bran, the more tasty they will be. The smaller the vegetables, the sooner they will pickle. Cover the container lightly to keep it clean and store in a cool place.

93

If the *nuka* (or flour) becomes too soft, add fresh roasted *nuka* or flour and some salt; only a little at time, or the taste is not so good.

For a more yin pickle, even apples can be pickled; but it would be best to use a separate container. These would be especially good for children but surely adults would like them as well.

After you remove the pickles, slice them in very small pieces, place in an attractive dish, and let everyone know that a small piece or two is sufficient, since these pickles are so salty.

We hope you enjoy making and eating these pickles.

おもしろい
味噌の使い方

Chapter 7

Miso for Fun

Pizza

Pizza Filling:

> Oil for sautéing
> 1/2 cup minced onions
> 1/2 cup chopped celery
> 1 cup parsnips, cut in large slices
> 2 cups carrots, cut in large slices
> Pinch of salt
> 1/2 cup mugi miso
> 1/2 cup water
> Teaspoon ginger juice or pinch of grated ginger
> 1/2 cup green pepper, sliced
> 1/2 cup scallions, sliced
> 1 cup tofu, cubed

Heat a pressure cooker, brush with oil and sauté vegetables in the following order: onion, celery, parsnips and carrot. Add water and a pinch of salt; cover and bring to pressure, and cook for 15 minutes.

Purée vegetables and blend with miso and ginger. Heat skillet, brush with oil, and lightly sauté the pepper and scallions. Blend with puréed vegetables and set aside.

Pizza Crust:

> 2-1/2 cups whole wheat pastry flour
> 1/2 teaspoon salt
> 1 cup water
> 1 tablespoon oil

Place 2 cups flour in bowl and mix in salt. Add oil and, with hands, rub into flour mixture. Beat dough until smooth and elastic. Add remainder of flour to make a stiff dough. Turn out onto a floured board and knead until smooth. Allow to stand 15 minutes.

Using half the dough at a time, roll into a circle and transfer to an oiled 13-inch pizza pan. Gently pull and stretch dough to fit pan and turn edges under to obtain a thicker edge. Spread filling over dough, top with *tofu* and bake in a pre-heated oven at 375 degrees for 30 minutes or until edges are slightly browned. Serve hot. Yields two 13-inch pizzas.

Variations for Pizza Filling:

Minced celery and/or parsley may be sautéed and added with onion.

Fresh fish (for example, shrimp or white-meat fish) may be placed on top of the pizza and baked with it.

Squash and onions can be substituted for the vegetables.

The variations are endless. Be creative, and try other vegetable combinations.

Miso Burgers

Yields 6 burgers:

2 cups cooked rice
1 scallion, cut in thin rounds
1 tablespoon tahini
1 minced onion
1 tablespoon miso
Oil for frying

Blend rice, scallions, *tahini*, onions and miso; then with lightly dampened hands form into patties.

Heat a skillet, brush with oil and fry burgers on a medium flame. Brown first one side and then the other. Serve on slices of bread with lettuce and pickle.

Grilled Miso Sandwiches

3 slices of bread
1/4 cup scallion-miso relish (see p. 72)
Oil for toasting

Evenly spread miso mixture over bread. Heat a skillet, brush with oil, and when it is warm, toast sandwich to desired crispness. Remove from skillet and cut into wedges.

Miso Bread

Miso acts as a fermenting agent in bread and produces a sweet-tasting, light bread. You may adapt any of your favorite bread or muffin recipes by replacing salt with miso.

8 cups whole-wheat flour
3 cups water
2/3 cup miso

Place flour in a mixing bowl. Purée miso with 1 cup water and add to the flour with remainder of water. Mix ingredients and knead for about 10 minutes or until a smooth, elastic texture is obtained. Place dough in a lightly oiled bowl and cover with a damp cloth. Allow bread to stand in a warm place overnight.

The next day, knead the bread again and form into two loaves. Heat bread pans and brush with oil. Place loaves in pans and cover with a damp cloth. Allow to rise in a warm place for 2 to 4 hours. Place in a cold oven and bake at 350 degrees for 1 hour and 15 minutes. Place a pan of cold water on the lower rack in the oven to assure even baking.

Variations:

Add only half of the miso and proceed as above. Before forming the dough into loaves, spread to a 1-inch thickness the length of the bread pans. Spread remainder of miso on top of the dough, roll up and place in pan. Bake as above. When the bread is sliced, the miso layer will form an attractive spiral.

For a richer-tasting bread, spread a thin layer of *tahini* over the miso layer. Please enjoy!

Miso Canapés

The watery consistency of cucumbers is beautifully balanced by miso. Slice a cucumber into ½-inch pieces and spread with a very thick layer of miso. Arrange with other vegetable garnishes and serve as finger food.

For delicious snacks, stuff pieces of celery with walnut-miso spread. (See p. 77—Miso Sauces and Spreads.) Also try raw fish with miso and a slice of grapefruit.

Miso Baked Apples

> **3 medium-sized apples**
> **2 tablespoons toasted and chopped walnuts**
> **2 tablespoons miso**
> **1/4 teaspoon grated lemon rind**

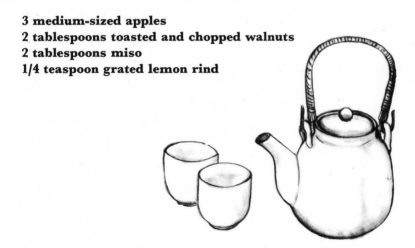

Cutting from the stem end, core apples. Blend miso, nuts and lemon peel and fill apple centers with the mixture. Place apples in an oiled baking dish, and bake in an oven preheated to 350 degrees, for 20 minutes.

Deep-fried Miso Balls

> **1 cup whole-wheat flour**
> **3/4 cup water**
> **2 medium minced onions**
> **1 tablespoon miso**

Add minced onions to flour and mix well. Dilute miso in ½ cup of water; add to flour mixture. Gradually add water to obtain a fairly dry dough. Drop by spoonfuls into deep hot oil and fry until they turn a deep golden color. Drain well.

Mince Pie

This rich pie adds the finishing touch to a Thanksgiving dinner.

Filling:

> **4 cups apple, cut in chunks**
> **2 cups raisins**
> **Pinch of salt**
> **3 cups water**
> **1/2 cup miso**
> **1 tablespoon grated orange rind**
> **1 tablespoon kuzu (or other thickening agent)**

Place apples, raisins, nuts and water in a pot, and add a pinch of salt. Cook with a cover over a medium-low flame for 3 to 4 hours. (To hasten the cooking, pressure-cook for 1 hour.) Remove ½ cup liquid, place in a bowl, add miso and purée. Add purée to pot and cook 15 minutes. Add orange juice and rind. Dilute *kuzu* in 3 tablespoons cold water; add to the pot and cook until the *kuzu* becomes clear. The flavor deepens if allowed to set for one day before serving.

Variation:

Carrots can be used instead of apples, and surprisingly, make a very good combination with raisins. This, of course, would make a more yang mince pie.

Pie Shell:

> **2 cups whole-wheat pastry flour**
> **1/2 teaspoon salt**
> **1/4 cup oil**
> **2/3 cup water**

Blend flour and salt together. Add oil and with your hands gently rub oil into flour mixture. Add water and quickly form a dough. For a light, delicate crust, work dough as little as possible with hands. Allow dough to relax for 10 minutes, then divide into halves and roll out on a floured surface. Line two 9-inch pie pans. Bake for 15 minutes in a 400-degree oven. Fill with mince filling and serve.

Basic Spaghetti Sauce with Miso

> **Makes 6 servings:**
>
> > **1 small beet (including greens)**
> > **4 chopped onions**
> > **4 to 5 carrots**
> > **1 green pepper**
> > **4 stalks of celery**
> > **2 tablespoons miso (rice miso is nice for this dish)**
> > **Oil for sautéings**

Chop beet greens, dice beets, slice carrots, green pepper and celery, and pressure cook together for 20 minutes. Sauté onion in a skillet until translucent and add to the other vegetables.

Mash all vegetables or use a food mill or blender. Add diluted miso and simmer for 5 minutes. Taste to see if you have enough miso. Serve over whole-wheat noodles.

Variations:

For Italian spaghetti add a pinch of oregano and pinch of basil.

Add sautéed mushrooms and/or *seitan* chunks.

The basic sauce can be used as a pizza spread for pizza.

Two tablespoons of *tahini* can be added to the sauce, plus any sautéed vegetables on top.

Tofu can also be added. When cooked, it has the taste and appearance of cheese.

There are really endless variations—add other vegetables like zucchini in the summertime, turnips in the winter. Experiment and see how creative you can be.

Chapter 8

Make Your Own Miso

Pounding Miso

After the golden fields of rice have been harvested, and the festival at the village shrine has quieted down, all the houses in the countryside begin to prepare for the coming winter. Now is the time of year when the autumn sun falls earlier and earlier into the west, as if it were a water bucket tumbling down into a well. The late autumn rains splash softly on the ground.

Each family prepares its own distinctive kind of miso: *kome* miso (rice miso), *mugi* miso (barley miso), *name* miso (salt and eggplant or melon), or *misozuke* (miso with pickled vegetables). When a family entertains neighbors and guests, the exchanging of different miso tastes is a part of friendship. Through miso the traditions of the family and the intimate efforts of the parents are automatically infused into the blood of the children, creating peace and health.

The Japanese compare miso-making to the cultivation of plants. They say that miso, like all living things, is an expression of the attitude, devotion, and sincerity of its creator.

The following *haiku* are poems about making miso. They spring from the lives of children who walk two or three miles each way to elementary school:

misomame no	*The smell of miso beans*
nioi takadaka	*soars high above*
ie no kado	*my house's gate*
chichi to haha ga	*Father and mother*
noshitari magetari	*flatten and then make a clump—*
misotsuki da	*it is miso-pounding!**
misotsuki ya	*Miso-pounding!*
soto wa akarui	*outside*
hangetsu da	*the bright half-moon*

All by Yoshiko Toya

---

* The miso is pounded with long wooden pestles.

Steps of Making Miso

Miso requires few ingredients, and can be easily made at home. Miso is prepared by a two-step fermentation process. The first step involves the fermentation of the grain or bean to produce enzymes and culminates in a product called *koji*. This is followed by a second fermentation period involving the *koji* plus soybeans and salt.

The First Step

Koji is fermented barley, rice, wheat or soybeans. Each type of miso takes its name from the kind of *koji* used. *Koji* digests the starches of grain and the protein of soybeans to produce a soluble product which is then fermented by yeasts and bacteria in the second stage of the process.

Although homemade *koji* is superior to store-bought *koji*, preparation requires a fermented starter called *tane koji*. Homemade *tane koji* can be made by cooking grain and innoculating it with the proper bacteria culture, but for beginners it is perhaps best to buy the commercial *tane koji*. At the present time, commercial *tane koji* is available from: American Type Culture Collection, 12301 Park Lawn Drive, Rockville, Maryland 20852, U.S.A. Ask for *koji* culture, aspergilus oryzae, Ahlburg Cohn, Code No. 14805. *Koji* is also available from Erewhon, Inc. in Boston.

Miso is then made by blending the *koji* with cooked soybeans and salt.

Homemade Barley Koji:

The following recipe is for barley *koji*, and calls for barley *tane koji*. It may be adapted for other types of miso by substituting rice, wheat or soybeans and their respective *koji* in place of barley and barley *tane koji*.

5 cups barley
10 cups water
1/2 cup barley tane koji

Wash barley in cold water and soak for 7 hours. Strain off water and steam barley in a wooden or stainless steel steamer for 1-½ hours until soft. Each grain should be dry and fluffy; that is why steaming is so important. Add more water if necessary during the steaming process.

Spread out the steamed barley in a large bowl and allow to cool to body temperature. Add ½ cup barley *tane koji* and mix well. Next spread out the steamed barley to only a 1-to 2-inch depth in a box of untreated natural wood if possible—at any rate, not a plastic container. Wrap the box with clean sheets, towels or a blanket and place in a warm room for 14 hours.

Check the mixture to see if the barley is slightly white and sticks to the box. This will indicate that the barley is working. Mix thoroughly and break lumps apart in order to maintain uniform temperature, moisture, and aeration. A temperature of 80 degrees should be maintained. It is advisable to have a pot of water on a hot-plate next to the boxes so that the steam keeps the mixture moist.

Cover again and then after 18 hours mix again. At this time the temperature will be around 105 degrees, and an aroma of fermentation will be obvious. After 45 hours, yellow-green fungi will appear, looking like flowers.

Chamber Fermentation

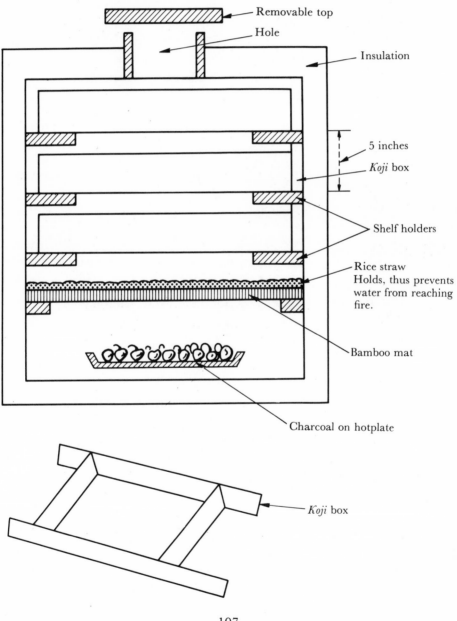

If any *koji* is left over, allow it to dry in the uncovered box. Thoroughly dried *koji* stores well and may be used as a miso ingredient or in other dishes such as *amazake*. The *koji* may also be reused once or twice as *tane* to make more *koji*, but since its bacterial count diminishes with each use, attempting a third batch from the original supply is not advised.

The Second Step

Soybeans

The main ingredient of miso is soybeans. Excellent domestic soybeans are available, and usually a yellow-white bean is recommended. (One special variety of miso calls for a black soybean which currently must be imported from the Orient.) All soybeans should be of vegetable, or edible quality, which differs from the type commonly fed livestock.

Salt

Salt acts as a preservative and exerts a selective action on the micro-organisms that flourish during fermentation. If salt were absent, a poisonous bacterial infestation would occur. High quality, minimally-refined sea salt should be used in order to establish a balanced mineral content of the miso.

The percentage of salt given in the table below is relative to the quantity of dry soybeans, not to the whole mixture of soybeans and *koji*. As a general rule, if you wish to produce a miso that will be ready to eat in a short time, use less salt. Miso doesn't spoil and its taste only improves with aging.

Minimum Aging Period Relative to Salt Content*

Salt Content	Minimum Aging Period
20% (1 cup)	3 months
30% (1½ cups)	6 months
40% (2 cups)	9 months
50% (2½ cups)	1 year
100% (5 cups)	3 years

Water

Good water is essential in the preparation of good miso. Avoid water containing chlorine, phosphates, or any type of additive. Untreated deep-well or spring water is recommended.

---

* The measurements given are for five cups of dry soybeans.

Some Kinds of Miso

Homemade Barley Miso

10 cups soybeans
30 cups water
5 cups salt
Barley koji

Pick out and discard all extraneous material, then wash soybeans in cold water and soak for overnight (or up to 17 hours) in a cool place. Good soybeans expand 2 to 3 times larger than their original size. Soybean soaking water should be changed once to avoid fermentation and sprouting.

Traditionally, soybeans were steamed in wooden boxes with bamboo slats until soft. If a wooden or stainless steel steamer is not available, then boiling the beans is advised. Using soaking water, boil beans with a drop top for 16 hours, adding more water as necessary. If pressure-cooked, allow 2 to 3 hours until very tender.

Allow to cool to room temperature. Drain off liquid and reserve. Remove beans gently from cooking utensil to a *suribachi* (mortar) for mashing. If a large quantity is being made, it is more practical to grind the beans in a grain mill on a very fine (tight) setting.

Mix with reserved liquid, which is a condensed form of soybean fat. Add salt, and mix thoroughly. Add barley *koji*, and mix thoroughly. Barley miso is usually 1 part *koji* to 1 part soybeans. Place the mixture in a wooden keg or earthenware crock, but do not fill it over 2/3 full, as the miso expands during aging.

To make miso sweeter, increase the *koji*; but if miso is made with 2 parts or more of *koji* to 1 part of soybeans, it does not keep well.

Place a one-layer covering of cloth such as muslin, cotton or linen on the miso, then cover with a wooden drop lid. Evenly distribute small stones on the lid to provide a little pressure. (The total weight of the stones should not exceed 1/7 of the total weight of the miso.) Cover with a piece of paper to keep out the dust. Store at room temperature. It is helpful to label the container, stating the ingredients, their proportions and the date.

After 10 days, uncover and mix well. Repeat this 2 more times at 10-day intervals. The fermentation period ends 2 ½ months from the time the *koji* was added. When that period is over the contents are removed to a different keg for aging. This step provides proper exposure to air and reduction of the miso's temperature.

Store in a cool place. Cover as before, and the miso will be ready for consumption following the proper aging period. During the fermentation and aging period you will note a progressive darkening of the miso and a change in its aroma. (See chart on p. 108).

Rice (Kome) Miso

In the making of miso, *koji* is used to change the soybeans' carbohydrates into a more digestible form. In rice miso this conversion is generally interrupted at the glucose stage. In barley miso, however, the conversion continues through to the alcohol stage. The alcohol gradually evaporates during the usual 2- to 3-year aging period, and the volume content of carbohydrates decreases proportionately. In rice miso, on the other hand, glucose and the carbohydrate volume content do not decrease with aging, while the water content does diminish.

Rice miso is prepared by following the barley miso recipe, simply substituting rice *koji* for barley *koji*.

Wheat Miso

Wheat miso has a special taste akin to that of *tamari*. Made in the same way as barley miso, wheat miso is especially good for pickling.

Mixed Grain Miso

It is not necessary to limit oneself to a one-grain *koji* in preparing miso. For a variety of flavors, a mixed *koji* of rice and barley, or of rice and wheat, may be used. To produce a mixed-grain *koji* adapt the barley *koji* recipe by using any proportion of two grains.

Kinzanji Miso

Invented in the Kinzanji Buddhist Temple in China, this is a table miso used in condiments, relishes, or salad dressings rather than in soup. It differs from other varieties in that a previously prepared *koji* is not used; rather, *tane koji* is added directly to the wheat-soybean mixture.

To make *Kinzanji Miso*, ingredients are used in the following proportions:

> **Dry soybeans: 2 parts**
> **Wheat: 1 part**
> **Salt: 1/3 of the amount of the soybeans**
> **Tane koji: 5% of the amount of the soybeans and wheat combined**

For example, if you wish to make a small batch of miso at home, the ingredients can be used in the following amounts:

110

Dry soybeans: 4 cups
Wheat: 2 cups
Salt: 1-1/3 cups
Tane koji: a scant 1/3 cup

Pick out extraneous material from beans; wash and drain. Toast over a low flame stirring continuously for 5 to 10 minutes. Mix soybeans and wheat together, and soak for 24 hours.

Cook beans and wheat together as described previously, until tender. Cool to body temperature. Mix the *tane koji* into the soybeans and wheat. Place this mixture in a wooden box and spread evenly to a depth of 1 inch. Wrap the box with clean towels or blankets and put in a warm place.

After 3 days, the mixture will begin to ferment, and at this point 1/3 of the salt should be added. After another 10 days, mix in another 1/3 of the salt; and again 10 days later, add the final 1/3 of the salt. After an additional 4 to 6 weeks of fermentation, the *Kinzanji Miso* is ready to eat.

For variety, any combination of the following ingredients may be introduced when salt is added: minced lemon peel, diced ginger, chopped *kombu*, salt pickles, eggplant, or cucumber.

Soybean (Hatcho) Miso

This miso has a simple taste and doesn't contain any grain, but it is very strengthening. Soybean miso is traditionally made in the Aichi-ken area of Japan, which is noted for its famous *samurai*. A *shogun* warrior from this land conquered Japan, and his family ruled for 400 years. The people of Aichi-ken credit this reign to the strong soybean miso they ate.

To prepare soybean miso, a soybean *koji* is required. It is made in the same way as barley *koji*. Blend soybean *koji* with a mixture of steamed soybeans and salt, as for the barley miso. For soybean miso, 30% to 50% *koji* is recommended per quantity of dry soybeans. *Koji* works more slowly on beans than on grain; 3 years' aging is recommended, and it may age up to 13 years.

During the aging of soybean miso, some liquid rises to its surface. This is the authentic *tamari*. Thus, soybean miso is less watery than other varieties of miso, and so it is especially good for making *tekka*.

Variation:

If a soybean *tane koji* is not available, it may be prepared after a primitive fashion. Cook soybeans as described above and form into balls the size of a fist. Store uncovered on racks in a warm, clean place for 7 months, and a natural fermentation will occur. Remove dust, mix and mash this natural starter with the appropriate proportion of salt and freshly cooked soybeans. Place in a keg, cover, store, mix, and age as for regular soybean miso.

111

Black Soybean Miso

Rich-tasting black soybeans produce a dark-colored miso which is delicious for miso pickles and salads.

Soak the black soybeans until they expand to about 2 ½ times their original size. Remove from water and steam until beans are somewhat soft (about 6 hours). Partially mash the beans in a *suribachi*. When cooled to body temperature, mix with rice *koji*, and proceed as for rice miso. One part black soybeans to one part rice *koji* is recommended.

Summary of Steps for Making Barley Miso

This is for miso of 50% *koji* and 50% salt to soybeans.

These proportions may be varied —see text for details.

(1)   Preparing the Ingredients

A. Koji

5 cups barley
10 cups water
1/2 cup barley tane koji

Wash barley.
Soak for 7 hours.
Strain out water.
Steam 1 hour.
Cool to body temperature.
Mix with ½ cup barley *tane koji*
Cover to keep warm.
Mix after 10 hours, and again after 18 hours.
Keep covered 45 hours.

B. Soybeans

10 cups soybeans
30 cups water
5 cups salt

Wash soybeans and soak for 24 hours.
Cook until tender.
Mash.

Mix with cooking water.
Add 5 cups salt.

(2) Fermentation and Aging

Mix A (*koji*) and B (soybeans) together.
Place in a keg; place stones on cover weighing 1/7 the weight of in-
   gredients.
Fermentation period:
Mix at 10-day intervals, three times.
45 days after mixing A and B, place in a different keg.
Aging period:
Miso is ready for consumption after 1 year aging.

We hope you enjoy making your own miso.

Glossary

Foods

Azuki Beans: A small red bean with a unique flavor. An import from northern Japan, *azuki* beans are said to be the best food for kidneys. Most yang bean.

Black Soybeans: A purple-black soybean. This rich-tasting bean is imported from Japan.

Bonito: A smoked, fermented, dried fish fillet. Flakes, taken from the fillet, give body to soup stocks and add a delicate fish flavor. To produce flakes, place the fillet in a damp towel for ½ hour to soften, then shave off desired quantity of flakes. A wooden shaving box is a convenient implement for storing and shaving the fish. Bonito may be purchased that is already flaked but for a much superior product buy the bonito fillet.

Buckwheat Groats: Whole buckwheat grains. Sometimes you can buy them already toasted, and sometimes untoasted.

Burdock or Gobo: A common wild plant with a black-skinned root. Burdock has a distinctive earth-like taste.

Daikon: A long white radish; when prepared well is very appetizing. *Daikon* lends itself well to miso soup and other vegetable dishes. Fresh, dried, or pickled *daikon* is available. Its yin qualities help to expel excess liquid. Grated and with a small amount of *tamari* added, it is often served as a side dish to aid digestion, especially with *tempura* or beans. In the summer, grated *daikon* helps to keep one cool.

Dulse: A delicate, tangy sea vegetable rich in minerals. Dulse is found on the eastern coastline of Canada.

Ginger: A yin root vegetable. Ginger pulp and juice is used in many food preparations. Fresh ginger is preferable to powdered.

Kanpyo: Dried gourd-strips. *Kanpyo* is used to tie cabbage, carrot or *kombu* rolls and in other vegetable preparations.

Kanten: A type of sea grass, sometimes called Japanese or vegetable gelatin; comes in bar form; also a powdered variety is available. It is used as a jelling agent in salads and desserts. It will jell without refrigeration.

Koji: A fermented grain or bean. *Koji* is an essential ingredient of miso, and is used in other food preparations.

Kombu: A sea vegetable high in iodine and trace minerals. *Kombu* has been used for over a thousand years as a flavoring for stock and also as a vegetable.

Kukicha Tea: Naturally grown tea made of three-year-old leaves and twigs of the *bancha* tea bush. *Kukicha* tea is a soothing beverage that aids digestion.

Kuzu: A wild plant related to the arrowroot family. The root, purchased in a white powdered form, is used as a thickening agent and for its strengthening, medicinal properties.

Lotus Root: The root of the lotus plant is used as a vegetable. Lotus has a crisp texture and unique flavor. It is traditionally used as a medicinal food for the lungs.

114

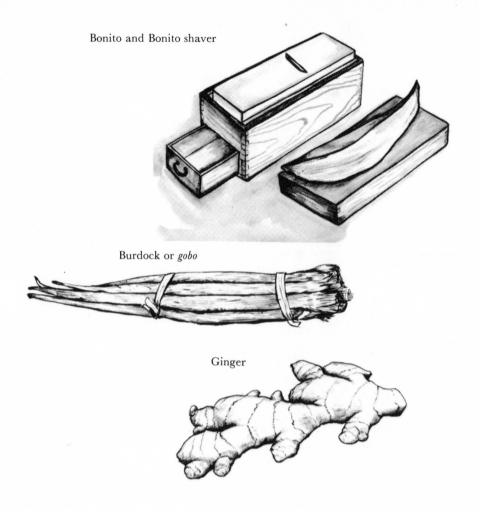

Bonito and Bonito shaver

Burdock or *gobo*

Ginger

Miso: An aged, fermented soybean purée containing living enzymes which aid digestion. Miso has a full-bodied taste and is a strengthening food. As a rule, miso is not boiled, for high temperatures destroy the enzymes. However, miso may be used as a flavoring agent, and then it is cooked into the dish.

Although miso stores best in a cool spot, it usually is not refrigerated, as refrigeration may destroy the living enzymes. Mold sometimes forms at the top of the container of miso, and this is simply an indication of its living quality. When mold occurs, simply blend it throughout the miso. There are some brands of chemicalized miso currently on the market. For your health, use only pure, traditionally made miso.

Mung Bean Threads: Chinese noodles, very thin and transparent, made of *mung* beans. Some bean threads are also made of rice or wheat and are called *vermicelli*. Gives a delicate effect to soups and vegetables.

Mushrooms: A very yin vegetable; therefore, the small, dried, more yang mushrooms called *shiitake* are recommended. Occasional use is suggested. The

115

shiitake mushroom is said to be good for discharging animal quality foods. Must be soaked for 20 minutes or more before using.

Nigari: Magnesium chloride or calcium chloride, used as a coagulating agent in making *tofu*. Naturally-produced *nigari* is made by hanging wet salt in a cloth bag; the moisture that drips from the bag is allowed to dry and used in a powder or flake form, and is much better quality than chemically-produced coagulants.

Noodle: Pasta made of flour, salt and water. Noodles made of wheat are called *udon*, and those made of buckwheat are called *soba*. Use noodles produced from a whole grain flour. Soy noodles are good for the summertime.

Nori: This Japanese dark mineral-rich sea vegetable comes in thin sheets. *Nori* is delicious used as a garnish. Toast *nori* by holding two sheets together and moving them rapidly back and forth above a medium flame. When the color becomes a lighter green, turn over and toast the other side. Then cut or tear into desired sizes and use as a garnish on soups, rice, noodles or vegetable dishes. Rice balls are delicious wrapped in *nori*.

Nuka: Rice bran.

Oil: Unrefined vegetable oil. This is a necessary ingredient for the preparation of many vegetable dishes. Lecithin, which is an important element for maintaining cellular life, is contained in unrefined vegetable oils. Sesame oil is a superior oil; corn and sunflower oils are also good.

Rice: A cereal grain. Organic, short-grain brown rice is the basis of the macrobiotic diet as it is the most completely balanced grain. It contains protein and many vitamins including Vitamin B-complex. Choose rice that is well-shaped and without chips or scratches. Rice is starch but its outer layers have the elements necessary to digest starch.

Sake·Lees (Kasu): A by-product sediment from the making of *sake*.

Salt, Sea: Sea salt contains an abundance of minerals and is produced by the evaporation of sea water. Toast salt before using to yangize it and this also eliminates the chlorine in the salt. To toast, place salt in a hot, dry skillet and stir continuously until it turns a deeper color. It is convenient to toast a week's supply at a time.

Sesame Seeds: Small, tan seeds with a rich flavor. Sesame seeds are high in protein and edible oil, and are an excellent source of phosphorous. Sesame seeds are toasted before using. To toast, first wash seeds and allow to drain for a few minutes. Heat a pan and on a medium-high flame roast the seeds, stirring continuously until their color turns a few shades darker and they emit a light aroma. Also, if a seed can be easily crushed between the ring finger and thumb it is adequately toasted. Immediately after toasting, pour seeds into a bowl to prevent scorching.

Sweet Rice: A variety of rice. In comparison with regular brown rice, sweet brown rice is slightly more soft, wet and sticky. Its sweetness is not like that of sugar, but rather, a mild grain sweetness. Sweet rice has been used traditionally in Japan to make special holiday cakes. When toasted, sweet rice puffs up a bit like popcorn.

Tahini: A paste, similar to peanut butter in consistency, ground from hulled sesame seeds. *Tahini* originated in the Middle East and is widely used there.

Prior to use, toast *tahini* in a dry skillet over a medium-high flame and stir continuously until it starts to brown. *Tahini* does not contain salt and therefore is combined with some form of salt before it is consumed.

Tane Koji: A fermented grain or bean product innoculated with a special mold. *Tane koji* is a necessary ingredient in the production of *koji*.

Tofu: A soybean product, known as soybean curd, white and cheese-like in texture. High in protein and in Vitamin B, it is somewhat bland in taste but when well-seasoned and combined with other foods, it is a gourmet item. It will keep only a limited time—about 2 weeks under refrigeration. Store it covered with water in a bowl or jar. *Tofu* available in Oriental grocery stores often contains chemicals so the homemade variety is best.

Tofu Lees: A by-product sediment from the making of *tofu*.

Umeboshi Plums: Plums pickled in salt for one year and sometimes flavored with *shiso* leaves. *Umeboshi* plums are excellent for digestion and have many other uses. These plums are an excellent source of salt.

Vegetables: Fresh and organically grown whenever possible.

Wakame Seaweed: *Wakame* seaweed shoots up its delicate green leaves in the late winter and early spring as the sea begins to warm. The first growth is a light and translucent frond which gradually darkens to a deep green. This is a sign of maturity and shows that the plant is rich in iodine and minerals. To prepare, soak and cut into small strips. It may then be added to miso soups or boiled with other vegetables. Also good soaked and uncooked with salads.

Whole Foods: Used to create lasting health. Whenever possible use fresh, whole foods that are grown naturally and without the use of chemical additives. Avoid frozen or canned foods.

Suggested Utensils

Bamboo Rice Paddles: Flat spatulas that come in a variety of sizes and are used for toasting grains, flours and seeds, and for serving foods. Bamboo paddles are a durable utensil and will prove to have many kitchen uses.

Chopsticks: Used for sautéing, deep-frying, serving and as eating utensils. For sensitive cooking use bamboo chopsticks. Japanese chopsticks are small with pointed tips, and are most often used as eating utensils. Chinese chopsticks are larger with square ends and are used as cooking utensils.

Colander: A perforated utensil used for washing vegetables and grains and for rinsing cooked pasta.

Crock: Large earthenware container. Crocks are used for preparing and aging miso and pickles.

Cutting Board: The cutting of vegetables is much easier with a board, and boards are useful for kneading flour products as well. There are good commercial varieties available, or any clean board can be used.

Drop Top: A lid that fits inside the pot and rests on the contents rather than on the pot's rim. A drop top is used for aging miso and pickles, and for preparing some vegetable and bean dishes. It provides a little pressure to the ingredients. In cooking, it allows steam to escape, and for aging foods it allows some air circulation.

Food Mill: A useful implement for puréeing cooked food. This inexpensive utensil is available at many hardware or department stores.

Grain Mill: Grinds grain, beans, seeds and nuts into varying textures. Flour is nutritionally superior when ground just prior to using, and the best way to assure having freshly ground flours is to grind them yourself. A grain mill is a good investment. Illustrated in this section is a hand mill which costs around $17.00. Electric mills are much more expensive.

Grater: A small-toothed, flat utensil of porcelain or stainless steel. This is used to pulverize vegetables and in this way the vegetable juice may be extracted. Porcelain is preferable, especially for medicinal use.

Keg: Large wooden container. Kegs are used for fermenting and aging miso and pickles.

Oil Skimmer: A lightly curved, fine-meshed strainer with a handle. An oil skimmer is used for removing bits of batter or grain from *tempura* oil.

Pressure Cooker: An airtight pot which cooks food under pressurized steam. This utensil is strongly recommended for preparing grains properly, and it may be used to cook beans and vegetables. It provides a more yang preparation than does pot cooking as nutritious elements do not escape with steam, and less liquid is required. A pressure cooker of stainless steel or enamel is preferred. Pressure cookers save time and are easy to use. Check that the escape valve is clear before placing the lid on and see that the lid fits securely. After pressure is up, indicated by the jiggling of the regulator, start to time the cooking period.

Skillet: A heavy cast-iron pan. A skillet gives the most satisfactory results for sautéing food, and when cared for properly will last a lifetime.

Soup Pot: A heavy pot of cast iron, enameled cast iron or stainless steel with a tight-fitting lid. Heavy cookware allows for more careful cooking. Yin materials such as aluminium or laminated pans should not be used.

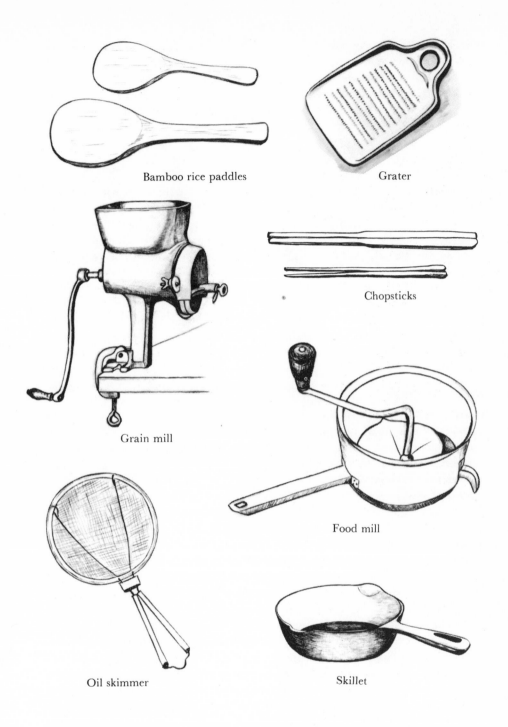

Bamboo rice paddles

Grater

Grain mill

Chopsticks

Food mill

Oil skimmer

Skillet

Suribachi: A serrated porcelain grinding bowl with a wooden pestle. Traditionally used for puréeing miso, vegetables, and for grinding seeds. It is a useful, practical, and peaceful utensil.

Vegetable Brushes: Made from sea vegetation, tightly bound with wire—excellent for cleaning roots and vegetables when you desire to leave the skin on.

Vegetable Knife: An essential kitchen tool. The Japanese knife with the squared-off end and double bevel is time-tested and most efficient. Carbon-steel knives hold a better edge than do stainless steel knives.

Wooden Spatulas, Spoons and Ladles: Used for stirring, sautéing and serving. With continual use, wooden implements become dry and may crack. To preserve their life, rub with vegetable oil.

Explanation of Terms Used

Dry Toast: To toast a seed, grain or flour in an unoiled skillet. Toast seeds and grains on a high flame and flours on a medium-low flame. To assure even toasting, stir quickly and continuously and remove the food from the skillet when it starts to brown. An alternate style of toasting grain is in a medium-high oven in an unoiled pan. Spread in a thin layer and check frequently to prevent over-cooking.

Sesame seeds require a special toasting technique which is described under sesame seeds in the list of foods.

Fire: A most important element in cooking. Of all animal life, man is unique as he alone can apply fire (yang) to his food and thus change his condition. The body assimilates cooked foods more easily than uncooked foods. Food cooked by yang fuel (most concentrated matter) is wood, next oil and then gas; electricity is very yin and microwave even more so—therefore, avoid these if possible. Yang fuel permits more careful food preparation since you can adjust the temperature to a finer degree.

Purée: To mash food in a mill, bowl, or *suribachi* to a smooth, even consistency.

Puréeing miso: To reduce miso to a texture that will allow it to easily blend with other ingredients. To purée miso place it in a bowl or *suribachi* and add enough liquid to make a smooth paste. Blend with a wooden pestle or spoon.

Sauté: A cooking method which utilizes a small amount of oil. To sauté, heat a pan or skillet, add oil and when it is warm at the sizzling stage, add vegetables. If too hot the vegetables cook too quickly and if not warm enough much nutrient is lost and the vegetables do not cook properly. If vegetables gently sizzle when added, then the oil is the right temperature for sautéing.

When sautéing soup vegetables, and especially miso soup vegetables, use a very small amount of oil, otherwise the soup will become heavy and unappetizing.

Vegetables sautéed on a high flame give greater strength than those cooked on a low flame. Stir only as necessary and sauté at least until the vegetable's color has changed and its aroma is released.

Tempura: In this traditional Japanese cooking method, foods are dipped in a thin batter, then deep-fried in about 2″ of hot vegetable oil. The resulting dish is delightfully crisp and delicious. Vegetables, fish, cooked grains and beans, and many other foods may be used.

Standard Tables of Food Composition

Compiled by Japan Nutritionist Association

The following food composition tables are for edible 100 grams. "A Activity" refers to precursors of Vitamin A which form into Vitamin A in the body, while "A" refers to Vitamin A preformed within the food.

Soybeans and Related Soybean Products I

	Cal.	Water g	Protein g	Fat g	Carbohydrates Sugar g	Carbohydrates Fibre g	Ash g	Calcium mg	Sodium mg	Phosphate mg	Iron mg
Soybeans dried, raw	392	12.0	34.3	17.5	26.7	4.5	5.0	190	3	470	7.0
Defatted soybeans	322	8.0	49.0	0.4	33.6	3.0	6.0	220	4	550	8.4
Roasted flour soybeans	426	5.0	38.4	19.2	29.5	2.9	5.0	190	4	500	9.0
Budo-name cooked	282	36.0	16.4	9.8	33.6	2.2	2.0	67	—	200	2.8
Soybean milk	42	90.8	3.6	2.0	2.9	0.2	0.5	15	2	49	1.2
Soybean curd ordinary	58	88.0	6.0	3.5	1.9	0	0.6	120	5	86	1.4
Kinugoshi tofu	47	89.7	4.9	2.8	1.5	0	1.1	150	(20)	56	1.1
Fukuroiri tofu	48	89.5	5.1	2.8	1.6	0	1.0	120	(20)	50	1.2
Roasted tofu	82	83.0	8.8	5.1	2.1	0	1.0	180	15	120	1.9
Aburage fried tofu	346	44.0	18.6	31.4	4.5	0.1	1.4	300	20	230	4.2
Nama-age fried tofu	105	79.0	10.1	7.0	2.8	0	1.1	240	(15)	150	2.6
Ganmodoki	192	64.0	15.4	14.0	5.1	0.1	1.4	270	—	200	3.6
Curd, congealed	436	10.4	53.4	26.4	7.0	0.2	2.6	590	18	710	9.4
Yuba	432	8.7	52.3	24.1	11.9	0	3.0	270	80	590	11.0
Okara	65	84.5	3.5	1.9	6.9	2.3	0.9	76	4	43	1.4
Natto	191	58.5	16.5	10.1	10.1	.2.3	2.6	92	—	190	3.3
Hama-natto	237	38.1	25.9	12.4	9.2	1.5	12.9	130	3,900	350	7.8

Soybeans and Related Soybean Products II

	A activity	A	Carotene	D	B₁	B₂	Nicotinic Acid	C	Remarks
	I.U.	I.U.	I.U.	mg	mg	mg	mg	mg	
Soybeans dried, raw	6	0	20	—	0.50	0.20	2.0	0	Includes domestic black and green soybeans
Defatted soybeans	0	0	0	—	0.45	0.15	2.0	0	
Roasted flour soybeans	5	0	15	—	0.40	0.15	2.0	0	
Budo-name cooked	0	0	0	—	0.05	0.03	0.4	0	Boiled
Soybean milk	0	0	0	—	0.03	0.02	0.5	0	
Soybean curd ordinary	0	0	0	—	0.02	0.02	0.4	0	
Kinugoshi tofu	0	0	0	—	0.02	0.02	0.3	0	
Fukuroiri tofu	0	0	0	—	0.03	0.02	0.3	0	
Roasted tofu	0	0	0	—	0.02	0.02	0.4	0	
Aburage fried *tofu*	0	0	0	—	0.02	0.02	0.5·	0	
Nama-age fried *tofu*	0	0	0	—	0.02	0.02	0.5	0	
Ganmodoki	0	0	0	—	0.01	0.03	1.0	0	
Curd, congealed	0	0	0	—	0.05	0.04	0.6	0	*Koya-dofu*
Yuba	20	0	60	—	0.20	0.08	2.0	0	
Okara	0	0	0	—	0.05	0.02	0.3	0	
Natto	0	0	0	—	0.07	0.56	1.1	0	
Hama-natto	0	0	0	—	0.08	0.11	0.1	0	Salt

Barley

	Cal.	Water g	Protein g	Fat g	Carbohydrates Sugar g	Fibre g	Ash g	Calcium mg	Sodium mg	Phosphate mg	Iron mg
Barley, whole grain	335	14.0	10.0	1.9	66.5	5.2	2.4	40	4	320	4.5
Whole grain, naked	337	14.0	10.6	2.0	69.7	1.9	1.8	40	3	340	3.0
Milled, pressed	337	14.0	8.8	0.9	74.7	0.7	0.9	24	3	140	1.5
Milled, cut	337	14.0	8.0	0.7	76.2	0.4	0.7	22	3	140	1.5
Roasted flour	344	12.0	10.8	2.0	70.6	2.6	2.0	42	3	350	4.5

Rice I

	Cal.	Water g	Protein g	Fat g	Carbohydrate Sugar g	Fibre g	Ash g	Calcium mg	Sodium mg	Phosphate mg	Iron mg
Rice, non-glutinous, brown	337	15.5	7.4	2.3	72.5	1.0	1.3	10	3	300	1.1
Half milled	345	Í5.5	6.9	1.5	74.5	0.6	1.0	7	2	200	0.7
Undermilled	350	15.5	6.6	1.1	75.6	0.4	0.8	6	2	170	0.5
Highly milled	351	15.5	6.2	0.8	76.6	0.3	0.6	6	2	150	0.4
Milled, imported	355	14.5	6.5	0.8	77.3	0.3	0.6	6	2	150	0.5

Rice II

	A activity I.U.	A I.U.	Carotene I.U.	D mg	B_1 mg	B_2 mg	Nicotinic Acid mg	C mg
Rice, non-glutinous, brown	0	0	0	—	0.36	1.10	4.5	0
Half milled	0	0	0	—	0.25	0.07	3.5	0
Undermilled	0	0	0	—	0.21	0.05	2.4	0
Highly milled	0	0	0	—	0.09	0.03	1.4	0
Milled, imported	0	0	0	—	0.06	0.03	1.4	0

Miso I

	Cal.	Water g	Protein g	Fat g	Carbohydrate Sugar g	Fibre g	Ash g	Calcium mg	Sodium mg	Phosphate mg	Iron mg
Sweet miso / Red miso / White miso (Salt 5.3%)	178	49.0	10.0	1.7	30.8	1.0	7.5	70	2,100	120	3.0
Light salty miso / Edo miso / Shinshu miso (Salt 10.4%)	158	50.0	12.6	3.4	19.4	1.8	12.8	90	4,100	160	4.0
Dark salty miso / Sendai miso / Country miso / Barley miso / Mugi miso (Salt 11.7%)	156	50.0	14.0	5.0	14.3	1.9	14.8	115	4,600	190	4.0
Mame miso / Hatcho miso / Nagoya miso (Salt 9.7%)	180	47.5	16.8	6.9	13.6	2.2	13.0	140	3,800	240	6.5
Powdered miso (Salt 18.5%)	303	5.0	23.6	9.0	32.2	3.6	26.6	180	7,500	320	8.0
Kinzanji miso	207	48.0	7.0	2.5	37.0	2.0	3.5	60		100	4.0
Sea bream miso	197	44.0	7.7	1.5	37.2	1.5	8.1	1,551	7,012	156	—
Tekka miso	249	40.0	9.0	5.2	40.8	2.0	3.0	150		250	60

Miso II

	A activity I.U.	A I.U.	Carotene I.U.	D I.U.	B_1 mg	B_2 mg	Nicotinic Acid mg	C mg
Sweet miso Red miso White miso (Salt 5.3%)	0	0	0	—	0.05	0.10	1.5	0
Light salty miso *Edo* miso *Shinshu* miso (Salt 10.4%)	0	0	0	—	0.03	0.10	1.5	0
Dark salty miso *Sendai* miso Country miso Barley miso *Mugi* miso (Salt 11.7%)	0	0	0	—	0.03	0.10	1.5	0
Mame miso *Hatcho* miso *Nagoya* miso (Salt 9.7%)	0	0	0	—	0.04	0.12	1.2	0
Powdered miso (Salt 18.5%)	0	0	0	—	0.05	0.15	2.0	0
Kinzanji miso	0	0	0	—	0.02	0.06	0.8	0
Sea bream miso	—	—	—	—	—	—	—	—
Tekka miso	0	0	0	—	0.10	0.15	1.5	0

Amino Acids Composition in Food I

	Protein	Isol.	Leu.	Lys.	Meth.	Cyst.	Pheny.	Try.	Thre.	Tryp.
Light salty miso	12.6	0.86	1.28	0.53	0.19	0.08	0.53	0.49	0.66	0.18
Dark salty miso	14.0	1.03	1.40	0.71	0.19	0.10	0.69	0.66	0.81	0.17
Mame miso	16.8	0.94	1.38	1.09	0.20	0.16	1.00	0.68	0.82	0.26

Amino Acids Composition in Food II

	Arg.	His.	Alen.	Asp. Acid	Glycine	Proline	Serine	Valine	Glutamic Acid
Light salty miso	0.73	0.31	0.73	1.43	0.60	1.04	0.73	0.75	2.16
Dark salty miso	0.78	0.37	0.76	1.69	0.66	0.98	0.88	0.86	2.40
Mame miso	1.09	0.47	0.74	1.94	0.71	1.21	1.06	0.97	3.53

Index